P9-DHC-699

Contemporary Studies in Literature

Eugene Ehrlich, *Columbia University*
Daniel Murphy, *City University of New York*
Series Editors

Volumes include:

WILLIAM FAULKNER, edited by Dean M. Schmitter

F. SCOTT FITZGERALD, edited by Kenneth E. Eble

ERNEST HEMINGWAY, edited by Arthur Waldhorn

D. H. LAWRENCE, edited by Leo Hamalian

WALT WHITMAN, edited by Arthur Golden

W. B. YEATS, edited by Patrick J. Keane

William Butler Yeats

a collection of criticism edited by Patrick J. Keane

McGraw-Hill Book Company

New York • St. Louis • San Francisco • London • Düsseldorf
Kuala Lumpur • Mexico • Montreal • Panama • Rio de Janeiro
Sydney • Toronto • Johannesburg • New Delhi • Singapore

821.8
Y3k

Copyright © 1973 by McGraw-Hill, Inc. All rights reserved. Printed in the United States of America. No part of this publication may be reproduced, stored in a retrieval system, or transmitted, in any form or by any means, electronic, mechanical, photocopying, recording, or otherwise, without the prior written permission of the publisher.

Selections from W. B. Yeats's *Collected Poems* are reprinted with permission of The Macmillan Company, copyright 1903, 1912, 1919, 1924, 1928, 1933, 1934, 1940 by The Macmillan Company; copyright 1940 by Georgie Yeats; copyright renewed 1931 by William Butler Yeats; copyright renewed 1940, 1947, 1952, by Bertha Georgie Yeats; copyright renewed 1956 by Georgie Yeats; copyright renewed 1961, 1962 by Bertha Georgie Yeats; copyright renewed 1968 by Bertha Georgie Yeats, Michael Butler Yeats, and Anne Yeats. Selections from W. B. Yeats's *Collected Plays* are reprinted with permission of The Macmillan Company, copyright 1934, 1952 by The Macmillan Company. Selections from *Mythologies* are reprinted with permission of The Macmillan Company, © 1959 by Mrs. W. B. Yeats; from *Essays and Introductions,* reprinted with permission of The Macmillan Company, © 1961 by Mrs. W. B. Yeats; from *Explorations,* reprinted with permission of The Macmillan Company, © 1962 by Mrs. W. B. Yeats. Excerpts from *The Letters of W. B. Yeats,* ed. Alan Wade, are reprinted with permission of The Macmillan Company, © 1953, 1954 by Anne Butler Yeats. Extracts from the *Letters* (acknowledgment also to Rupert Hart-Davis), poems, plays, and prose of W. B. Yeats are reprinted by permission of A. P. Watt & Son, London; M. B. Yeats; Macmillan & Co.; and The Macmillan Company of Canada.

Selection from "Little Gidding" in *Four Quartets* by T. S. Eliot, copyright, 1943 by T. S. Eliot; copyright, 1971, by Esme Valerie Eliot. Reprinted by permission of Harcourt Brace Jovanovich, Inc., and Faber and Faber, Ltd., Publishers.

Selections from *The Portable Nietzsche* edited by Walter Kaufmann, copyright 1954 by The Viking Press, Inc., reprinted by permission of The Viking Press, Inc.

123456789MUMU79876543

74.9-929

Library of Congress Cataloging in Publication Data

Keane, Patrick J comp.
William Butler Yeats

(Contemporary Studies in Literature)
Contents: Jeffares, A. N. W. B. Yeats.—Kermode, F. The suffering man, the creative mind.—Keane, P. J. Embodied song. [etc.] Bibliography (p.)
1. Yeats, William Butler, 1865–1939—Addresses, essays, lectures.
PR5907.K4 821'.8 72-10462
ISBN 0-07-033424-2

HIGHLAND COMMUNITY
JUNIOR COLLEGE LIBRARY
HIGHLAND, KANSAS

Contents

Patrick J. Keane

Introduction

I

More than sixty years ago, Ezra Pound set out to discover "how Yeats did it." He has been followed. The flow of critical material, having peaked during the centennial year (1965), has hardly abated. (One Yeats bibliography published in 1971 is aptly entitled *The Great Deluge.*) New readers, their innocence not yet drowned in that ink-stained tide, are perhaps to be envied. Yet what Blake calls "Unorganized Innocence" is no more adequate than Socrates' "unexamined life"; and besides, the secondary literature is unavoidably *there.* Helped, but also threatened by this critical inundation, students must attend those who, like the goldsmiths of Byzantium, "break the flood."[1] The central sections of this volume gather together at least some of the gold of a handful of our best contemporary smithies—major critics who have fixed, if not quite completed, our image of the greatest poet to have written in English in this century.

In selecting and arranging the essays and excerpts that follow, I have tried to be both helpful to readers and faithful to Yeats. A further word about that.

The convergence of certain characteristic tendencies of Yeats—his architectural arrangement of poems within a meaningful context, his infinite variations on a limited number of central motifs, the organization of recurrent images throughout his work —produces what Northrop Frye calls a "cosmology," a cohesive, symmetrical whole subsuming its parts. This, in turn, produces both an opportunity and a danger. The danger lies in the possible

[1] *CP,* 244. References to Yeats's works are keyed, throughout the present volume, to the table of abbreviations given in the "Note on Documentation" at the end of this Introduction.

subordination of individual poems to the "vast design"[2] of which they are "only" parts. Despite the insistence of the "New Critics" on the autonomy of each poem, the bulk of Yeats criticism, fulfilling the prophecy Allen Tate made thirty years ago, moves away from attention to "the poetry itself."[3] The work of the past two decades has not really filled that "one surprising gap" ("a thorough analysis of Yeats's verse as verse") noted by the editors of the important watershed collection, *The Permanence of Yeats* (1950). A hundred books and a thousand articles after Pound, we are still wondering "how Yeats did it."

This situation would have amused and appalled the poet, who worked hard to drag into being all that loveliness. But he is hardly blameless. Quite aside from his creation of major poems whose mysterious power defies analysis and exquisite lyrics whose music brings exegesis to its knees, the pseudophilosophical dragon at the mouth of the cave, *A Vision,* is also there to remind us that his "System"—"those hard symbolic bones under the skin" (*V,* 24)—meant almost as much to him as, say, "Among School Children's" "body swayed to music" (*CP,* 214). We may agree with one of the critics (W. Y. Tindall) that "a little" of Yeats's System "seems too much, his business none of ours," and yet grant that he knew his business. Most of the poems can be read independently of *A Vision,* but they could not have been *written* without those "stylistic arrangements of experience" that enabled Yeats, as he said, "to hold in a single thought reality and justice" (*V,* 25); without, that is, his imposition of an overarching schematic order upon the chaos of the actual.

Trying to hold all in a single thought, in the one completed symbol, Yeats is a poet whose work does approach the total integration of that "sacred book of the arts" he spoke so much about. "I must leave my myths and symbols to explain themselves as the years go by, and one poem lights up another," he said in 1901 (*VP,* 847); and he strove always to obey the injunction: "Hammer your thoughts into unity" (*Ex,* 263). Context, then: within the body of his own work and within the literary tradition itself. For Yeats was an "architect," and a traditionalist acutely conscious both of

[2] *V,* 280. Unfortunately, Yeats's own "design" is somewhat marred by the editorial ordering of pieces in the posthumous *Last Poems*—a volume which Yeats intended to begin, not end, with "Under Ben Bulben."

[3] Shortly after the poet's death Tate warned that in a period of growing interest in so massive an achievement, "Yeats's special qualities will instigate special studies of great ingenuity, but the more direct and more difficult problem of the poetry itself will probably be delayed." Tate's essay is included in Steinmann and Hall (see Bibliography).

his literary heritage and of the Neoplatonic, occult "Tradition." Finally, he was a poet who drew his images "out of *Spiritus Mundi*" (*CP,* 185)—that general storehouse of the collective unconscious—and so provides fertile ground for the archetypalist.[4]

Hence, the critical "opportunity" mentioned above. Indeed, in a volume where there is insufficient space for detailed consideration of many individual poems and plays,[5] the contextual and archetypal approaches—the most effective methods of illuminating the total "world" of a poet like Yeats—are precisely what is needed. And if we remember, too, that the chaos of "reality" not only generates but threatens the order of "justice"; that it was not Yeats but his "Plato" who "thought nature but a spume that plays/ Upon a ghostly paradigm of things" (*CP,* 214); that Yeats, committed to *both* spume and paradigm, natural root and heavenly blossom, was not the sort of poet who, having attained the topmost rung, kicks the physical ladder away; that he not only insists on the inextricability of the individual figure and the symbolic pattern ("How can we know the dancer from the dance?"), but even emphasizes the cold comfort of archetypal "justice" and cyclical recurrence in the face of such a human "reality" as the death of a beloved friend—"I am in despair that time may bring/ Approved patterns of women or of men/ But not that selfsame excellence again" (*CP,* 317)—if we remember all this, and then include critics sufficiently alert to the seductions of architecture, and especially of archetype, to assert allegiance to the particular and the unique, we cannot grievously miss our way.

This, then, was what I meant by fidelity to Yeats, a poet whose art consists of unique poetic embodiments of certain recurrent patterns, and whose perspectives range from the microscopic (painful, much-revised labor on the half-dozen or so lines that represented at the height of his powers a good day's work)[6] to the telescopic (the God's-eye view of a man absorbed in the vast, remote cycles—the "gygantogyres"—of *A Vision*). Between these Yeatsian extremities, his critics, too, must run their chosen

[4] See Hugh Kenner's essay (reprinted in the collection edited by Unterecker), as well as the books listed in the Bibliography by Donald Stauffer, John Unterecker, Harold Bloom, and F. A. C. Wilson, among others. Northrop Frye's essays on Yeats are mentioned below.

[5] While the plays, which have received considerable attention in recent years, are dealt with only peripherally in the essays that follow, much of the thematic commentary is applicable to them as well as to the poems.

[6] Yeats's working manuscripts have been examined in detail. See Richard Ellmann, *The Identity of Yeats,* and the books listed in the Bibliography by Jeffares, Parkinson, Bradford, and Stallworthy.

courses; and, if any message is clear, it may be—beyond Frank Kermode's "when you hear talk of archetypes, reach for your reality principle"—simply: "reach for both." For as Yeats himself said, he wrote poems in which "an always personal emotion was woven into a general pattern of myth and symbol" (*A*, 101–2).

"An aimless joy is a pure joy," according to one Yeatsian *persona* (*CP*, 139). If so, the present volume is impure, for it has not (to raid *Finnegans Wake* again) been "whorled without aimed." I've tried to impose on the book a focal scheme in keeping with Yeat's own "widening gyre" of commitments: to the individual poem; to the particular volume of which it is a part; to the canon in which that volume takes its place; to the literary tradition—"We were the last romantics" (*CP*, 240)—within which and against which Yeats worked; and, finally, to the world of paradigm and archetype which lured him, supplied him with images, and often repelled him.

II

The book falls into three parts, the first introductory and centering on what might be called the connection, distinction, and reconnection between Yeats's life and work. Although T. R. Henn and Richard Ellmann rival his knowledge, it would be hard to think of anyone more familiar with Yeats's life than A. Norman Jeffares, the author of *W. B. Yeats, Man and Poet.*[7] We have no room here for the intimate details with which Jeffares's mind is so richly stocked, but, as his biographical sketch shows, familiarity can also breed succinctness. Recalling, and linking, his personal responses to the deaths of Yeats and T. S. Eliot, Frank Kermode offers, in the next brief selection, useful observations on the relationship between "the man who suffers" and "the mind that creates." His theme and reference to "Cuchulain Comforted" are elaborated in my own essay. Employing wherever possible the poet's own words and images, I concentrate on the connection between man and poet, Yeats's life and work, and the connection between his two "worlds"—their opposing "masked" spokesmen, their underlying interdependence, and their final symbolic integration in an "embodied song" completed by Yeats on his deathbed.

After this preliminary overview, the main body of the book moves from close attention to particular—and particularly central

[7] As the present volume goes to press, what promises to be the definitive biography of Yeats, by Denis Donoghue, is soon to appear.

—poems, through a middle-range perspective, until, finally, we find ourselves "standing back" (to employ Northrop Frye's own visual analogy) at the distance of archetypal criticism. We have, therefore, intrinsically excellent Yeats commentary written by some of the dominant figures in post-World War II literary criticism combined with a graduated range of critical perspectives.

This arrangement, and the quite different approaches of the critics chosen, should help readers "into" Yeats. For example, while our final critic, Frye, has been accused (elsewhere, but by some of those included in this volume) of emphasizing systematic "structure" at the expense of the particularity and "texture" of individual poems,[8] it is precisely this close attention that is the forte of M. L. Rosenthal and Balachandra Rajan. Hence we begin with excerpts from their excellent introductory studies of Yeats: "intrinsic" discussions, in which attention is directed to the concrete details and inner dynamics that make a poem "work," of specific embodiments of two of Yeats's recurrent themes. Rosenthal addresses himself to the complex interplay between reality and imagination, the Here and the There, in "The Stolen Child," "The Man Who Dreamed of Faeryland," "The Lake Isle of Innisfree," "Who Goes with Fergus?" and "Sailing to Byzantium"; Rajan, to the theme of violent apocalypse in "No Second Troy," "The Second Coming," and "Leda and the Swan."[9]

Focusing on perhaps the two greatest "public" poems of our century, C. K. Stead and T. R. Whitaker explore Yeats's imaginative participation in, and aesthetic distancing from, the violent political events on which they are based. Stead discusses "Easter 1916" as a "symbolic gesture," an employment of "the terms of drama in order to stylize and objectify the world of political fact

[8] "To disagree with it," Frank Kermode wrote of Frye's *Anatomy of Criticism,* "is almost physically painful, though very necessary, [for] it fails, or refuses, to convey anything of what might be called the personal presence of any of the thousands of works discussed." Just as he values Yeats not for the "System," but for what happens in the poems, Kermode approaches Frye looking "for a way of saving some of the insights without accepting the doctrine; exactly what Frye regards as an impossible compromise." Denis Donoghue, too, though he admires Frye ("a dazzling critic, a joy to watch, a great athlete") has a "real quarrel" with him: "Even when he has dealt with the myth, structure, genre, and convention, I still find that he has left me somewhat short of the poetry. Structure is fine, but what about texture?" The difference, as my synopsis of Donoghue's position below would indicate, is philosophical as well: Frye is "interested in 'the kind of thing that happens all the time'; I, in the particular thing that happened at one particular time."

[9] In an essay too long to include here, the distinguished scholar Leo Spitzer approaches "Leda and the Swan" as "an incomparable unique poetic entity in itself." His concern (exceeding even that of Rosenthal and Rajan) is for "the most individual, the least cataloguable features of a poem."

which is its subject." Whitaker examines "Nineteen Hundred and Nineteen" as a poem combining the perspectives of "dramatic experience and panoramic vision," the shifting double view which is the major theme of his rich (source- and analogue-laden) synthesis of Yeatsian thought, *Swan and Shadow.*

Part III, comprising half the book, is given over to four of the least dispensable critics of our time.

Tied to no critical dogma, Frank Kermode has allegiances only to the historical-literary tradition itself and to the particular work he is examining. He chose to examine the work of Yeats in *Romantic Image,* an enormously influential, often misread study of the modern culmination of the romantic-symbolist tradition. Misread because, as that book and his subsequent volumes demonstrate, Kermode, like Edmund Wilson, has grave misgivings about the occult, irrational, isolating, antidemocratic ramifications of symbolism. But Kermode is, above all, faithful to the work at hand. Thus, we sense few of these reservations in the course of his brilliant discussion of the historical background and Yeatsian employment (in "Among School Children" and "The Two Trees") of two of the central romantic-symbolist icons, Tree and Dancer.[10]

The recurrence of certain central ideas and symbols is also the theme of Richard Ellmann, whose three Yeats volumes make him still *il maestro di color che sanno* among Yeatsians. As poem-oriented as Kermode's, Ellmann's essay (chapter 3 of *The Identity of Yeats*) places even greater emphasis on the poet's personal handling of symbolist theory. Ideas must neither be ignored nor tightly gripped as "beliefs"; they must be "overpowered" and then embodied within the dramatic context of the particular poem—serving the poem, which always "comes first."

Selecting five "recurrent ideas" in Yeats's verse, Ellmann discusses their poetic and symbolistic deployment, once they have been subordinated to what Yeats called the "moods." "Ideas which

[10] Excerpting portions of so tightly argued a volume as *Romantic Image* is hardly fair to Kermode. It should at least be noted that he uses that term throughout in a clearly defined sense. The poem, he writes (p. 43), is

> one of those victories by which the artist lives in tragic solitude. He reconciles the opposites of action and contemplation; and this reconciliation of opposites, very proper in a Romantic poet, is the purpose of the Yeatsian symbol, which is the flowering of what I call the Romantic Image. (. . . "Romantic" in a restricted sense, as applicable to the literature of one epoch, beginning in the late years of the eighteenth century and not yet finished, and as referring to the high valuation placed during this period upon the image-making powers of the mind at the expense of its rational powers, and to the substitution of organicist for mechanistic modes of thinking about works of art.)

Within this context, the excerpts may stand on their own.

occur in moods are 'lived' and lose their abstractness," writes Ellmann; "beliefs are dramatized and lose their affiliations with dogma to take on affiliations with the dramatic speaker of the poem." Thus the "moods" and their appropriate masks exempted Yeat's poetry from both "conventional beliefs" and "fashionable doubts," and made "forceful asseveration possible to a man whose point of view was flexible." The result: poetic "assertion" without ideological "doctrine," and an emphasis on human experience rather than abstract, or even symbolist, theory.

Whereas Kermode emphasizes (with certain qualifications) Yeats's role as a symbolist, and Ellmann personalizes it, a more recently emerged major critic, Denis Donoghue, minimizes, even flatly denies it: "Yeats was not a Symbolist."[11] Though he has reservations about mood and mask (noting the limitations as well as the strengths of the poet's temporary adoption of extreme perspectives and postures), Donoghue, like Ellmann, focuses on human experience and on that tense, dramatized vacillation which is the mainspring of Yeats's poetic power. With full awareness of the mediating power of myth, Yeats (Donoghue argues persuasively) is committed predominantly to what he himself called "the cycle that carries us into man," the "antithetical" way of the "Self." For all his Byzantinism, Yeats's focus was upon *this* world, living experience, the "human image."

We come, finally, to the most-discussed critic in the English-speaking world. Having cracked the symbolic code of Blake's Prophetic Books in *Fearful Symmetry,* Northrop Frye directed his energies to the establishment of a systematic and comprehensive criticism. The result, *Anatomy of Criticism,* has been the object of awe, admiration, and attack; frequently—as the previously noted reactions of Kermode and Donoghue demonstrate—of all three at once.

Of course, Kermode and Donoghue also chart the crucial symbols in the work of a poet like Yeats; but whereas Frye's concern is with the schematization of the multitudinous ways in which the recurrent is embodied, theirs (and Ellmann's) is with the "particular" poetic embodiments themselves. As I said at the outset, our concern, if we would be faithful to Yeats, must be, like his, with both. Yeats found room for "texture" *and* "structure," body *and* skeleton, personal particularity *and* recurrent mythic pattern, and so must we. Thus, while it is always an enriching

[11] In Donoghue's more recent book, *William Butler Yeats* (Viking Press, New York, 1971), Yeats is described as "an equivocal Symbolist, if not a lapsed member of the faith" (p. 106).

experience to read him, it is particularly rewarding to read Frye on Yeats—a poet who rewards the archetypal approach, who shares Frye's roots in apocalyptic romanticism, whose superb early essay on Shelley's recurrent image clusters has in fact served as one of the models for Frye's own work.

That work, wide-ranging and immense as it is, rotates (like Yeats's) in just a few orbits—as Frye not only admits but claims. It is hardly surprising, therefore, that over the past quarter-century the orbits have frequently coincided, the relevant full-scale essays being "Yeats and the Language of Symbolism" (1948), "The Rising of the Moon: A Study of *A Vision*" (1965), and "The Top of the Tower: A Study of the Imagery of Yeats," a paper delivered at the 1968 Yeats Conference in Sligo, first published in *Southern Review* in 1969, and since described by Frye as his "third effort, which by folk-tale convention ought to be the most successful one, to reconcile Yeats's imagery as a whole with the scheme of *A Vision.*"

III

Having read these essays and excerpts, preferably in the order of arrangement, we will find ourselves, I think, agreeing with Blake (and Yeats) that "without contraries is no progression," and that there's more than one way to skin the poet who gaily called himself "king of the cats." And despite this surgical image, we needn't worry that we "murder to dissect." Yeats and his poems survive the acutest critical scalpels; in fact, the "Yeats industry" might well quote A. E. Housman in one collective voice: "Ten thousand times I've done my best,/ And all's to do again." As in his poem "The Scholars" (*CP,* 139), Yeats has the last laugh at those who would annotate his lines; but he wanted annotation, began the parade himself, and, from beyond that grave under Ben Bulben, spurs on not only the horseman but the critic.

The essays by Kermode, Rosenthal, Rajan, Stead, Whitaker, and Donoghue have been gathered from larger works and in one case from more than one work. The titles used for these excerpts in the present volume have been supplied by the editor to provide the reader with a more precise designation of the content than to be found in the original source. Original sources are noted at the foot of the opening page of each previously published essay.

A NOTE ON DOCUMENTATION

Footnotes in the present volume, unless otherwise indicated, are mine. Of the critics represented, only Whitaker and Ellmann systematically cite sources or elaborate points made in their texts. Most of the critics do not (to paraphrase "Lapis Lazuli") break up their lines to cite. The essays, particularly those in Part III, are richly allusive. In general, I have tried to steer a middle course between cluttering up their essays and helping students locate unidentified quotations from and allusions to Yeats's work, particularly the poetry and plays. To save space, most such citations have been incorporated within the text in brackets (in the case of my own material, in parentheses), using the following abbreviations for the standard Yeats works (for precise information on the editions, consult the Bibliography at the end of this volume):

A *The Autobiography of William Butler Yeats*
CP *The Collected Poems of W. B. Yeats*
CPl *The Collected Plays of W. B. Yeats*
E&I *Essays and Introductions*
Ex *Explorations*
L *The Letters of W. B. Yeats* (ed. Allan Wade)
M *Mythologies*
V *A Vision* (2nd ed., 1937)
VP *The Variorum Edition of the Poems of W. B. Yeats* (ed. Peter Allt and Russell K. Alspach)

Part I

A. Norman Jeffares

W. B. Yeats

William Butler Yeats (1865–1939) was the eldest son of John Butler Yeats, whose family probably came to Ireland from Yorkshire at the end of the seventeenth century. It was intended that John Butler Yeats should follow his father's and grandfather's example and enter the Church of Ireland; but when an undergraduate he turned sceptic and, after trying the law, became an artist. He moved his household several times between Dublin and London, and as money was often scarce, his children spent a good deal of time in Sligo, in the west of Ireland, where Mrs. Yeats's parents, the Pollexfens, were well-to-do merchants. W. B. Yeats went to the Godolphin School in Hammersmith, and later to the High School in Dublin. He then studied at the School of Art in Dublin, where a fellow student, George Russell (AE), became his friend and shared his interest in mystic religion and the supernatural. He began to write poetry in his late teens with his father's enthusiastic encouragement.

His poetry began by echoing Shelley and Spenser and the pre-Raphaelites. His aims were to write for an Irish audience and about Ireland—to re-create a specifically Irish literature. At first he drew upon the fairy and folk tales which he had heard in the West of Ireland, and which he subsequently traced in printed material. In the poems of *The Rose* he began to use material from the Gaelic legends, the Cuchulain saga and the tales of the Fianna, which he read in nineteenth-century translations. He was active in creating the movement known as the Irish Literary Renaissance.

Introduction to W. B. Yeats: Selected Poetry, *edited by A. Norman Jeffares, pp. xiii–xxi. Copyright © 1962 by A. Norman Jeffares and Macmillan & Co., Ltd. Reprinted by permission of Macmillan (London and Basingstoke).*

After Parnell's death in 1891 there seemed an opportunity to draw youthful national feeling to a movement with a non-political aim, and so he busied himself founding literary societies, making speeches, and writing articles and reviews in papers and journals, in order to create a public sympathetic to his ideas and hopes for a distinctively Irish literature.

During the eighties and nineties heterodox religious movements claimed much of Yeats's interest in his search for some system in which he could believe. His father's rationalism and the aftermath of the Darwinian controversy had precluded him, he said afterwards, from accepting orthodox Christianity, and he explored instead Theosophy, Rosicrucianism, Platonism, Neo-Platonism, the writings of Swedenborg and Boehme and above all Blake, whose works he edited with Edwin Ellis during 1891–93. He turned to spiritualism, even to magic, but always, even in the midst of this search for belief, his mind remained partially sceptical, ironic, even potentially mocking.

He took an increasingly active interest in nationalist politics, at first under the influence of John O'Leary, an old Fenian leader who had spent many years in exile in Paris, and later of Maud Gonne. She was the daughter of an English colonel and had become a revolutionary. She was a superbly beautiful woman with whom Yeats fell in love when he first met her at the age of twenty-three. He realised his literary aims and activities were not likely to impress Maud Gonne, who was in favour of violent action. He therefore became deeply engaged during 1897 and 1898 in a political movement intended to unite different nationalist elements in Ireland; he even joined the secret extremist revolutionary Irish Republican Brotherhood for a time.

The poetry Yeats wrote during these crowded years—when he was poor, establishing himself by contributions to journals and fighting to create a public for Irish literature—reveals little of his own life beyond the unhappiness of his defeatist, unrequited love affair. His poetry became steadily more elaborate, more "mysterious and inscrutable," during the nineties, as he distilled his essences of mournful spiritual beauty. By the publication of *The Wind Among the Reeds* in 1899 he had moved a long way from his early desire to write popular poetry. He had gone through a period of learning his craft, discussing technique with his fellow members of the Rhymers Club (which met in a Fleet Street public house, The Cheshire Cheese), poets of the nineties who included Lionel Johnson, John Davidson, and Ernest Dowson. And now, influenced by what his friend Arthur Symons, the critic, had told him of the symbolists, of Verlaine and Mallarmé, and by the work of Villiers de l'Isle-Adam and Maeterlinck, he was writing intense yet rarefied poems, delicately beautiful and weakly adjectival. He was bringing his early work of the Celtic Twilight period to its fullest, most elaborate development.

This style changed, gradually at first, as his next volume, *In the Seven Woods* (1903), indicates by the new tone of its love poetry, which is more personal and realistic. But in 1903 Maud Gonne married John MacBride, another revolutionary, and Yeats was deeply hurt. Now he could merely record memories and old hopes, paying tribute to her great beauty—and his own celebration of it. In a superb series of poems ("Words," "A Woman Homer Sung," "No Second Troy") in *The Green Helmet and Other Poems* (1910) he compares her to Helen. She is without blame, for she is, like Helen, beyond praise or comment. This volume indicates an almost complete transition of style, for here Yeats introduces topical affairs and his own views and beliefs, as well as recording the emptiness of his passion. The poems are simple, even flatly prosaic at times, for Yeats was preoccupied with "theatre business, management of men" [*CP*, 91]. He had become disillusioned with Irish politics and politicians largely as a result of his experiences with the '98 Association and the I.R.B., and he had returned to a long-held ambition of creating an Irish theatre. He was helped in this by Lady Gregory, the widow of an Anglo-Irish landowner. He first met her at Coole Park, her house in County Galway, in 1896, and the following year he spent the first of many summers there. It was an ideal place for him to recover his health from the incessant emotional and financial strains of previous years, and Lady Gregory provided him with an ideal ambience—he helped her to collect folk-lore, he lived a regular life, he came to develop a belief in the virtues of both aristocratic and peasant life. And, with Lady Gregory's practicality and determination to aid him, he brought a national theatre into being.

In the first years they were aided by Edward Martyn, a neighbouring landowner, and George Moore, whose brief association with the Irish literary movement is told so well in *Ave, Salve, Vale.* The play Yeats had earlier written for Maud Gonne, *The Countess Cathleen,* was performed in 1899; other plays followed, and in 1902, when Martyn and Moore had dropped out of the movement, *Cathleen ni Houlihan,* the supreme expression of Yeat's early nationalism—and love—was performed with Maud Gonne in the title rôle. When the Abbey Theatre was established in 1904 Yeats became its production manager until 1910. This was an unselfish rôle, for the theatre moved away from his own ideals of poetic drama towards the realistic work of other, younger dramatists. A further piece of unselfishness was his spirited defence of Synge's play, *The Playboy of the Western World,* in 1907. He had met Synge in Paris in 1896 and had urged on him the idea of visiting the Gaelic-speaking Aran islanders and making them the subject of his writing. Synge had become a co-Director, with Lady Gregory and Yeats, of the limited company which replaced the previous national theatre in 1905; his work was unpopular with nationalist opinion, which regarded the *Playboy* as a slur on Irish manhood. Yeats courageously insisted on continuing the play despite hostile audiences, but in the process he became even more disillusioned by his "blind, bitter land" [*CP,* 88].

His next volume of poems, *Responsibilities* (1914), contains an entirely changed poetry, the antithesis of his early work, stripped of its decoration and mystery. In this he turned to savage satire and invective, defending great art against the philistines. Synge and Sir Hugh Lane (Lady Gregory's nephew) stand as his symbols of the artist and the enlightened patron. Lane's offering his collection of pictures as a gift to Dublin (on condition that a suitable gallery be built to house it) had not been properly appreciated, just as Synge's art had been despised by Dublin. Yeats began to praise the refinement and public-spiritedness of aristocratic life, drawing images from the great Renaissance patrons of Italy, and he also veered to the other extreme, of a gusty enjoyment of coarseness in the poems he wrote about beggars. He repudiated all the Celtic Twilight's "embroideries out of old mythologies" in "A Coat"; he recorded his disillusionment with the realities of Ireland in "The Fisherman"; and he inveighed against her ingratitude to her benefactors in "To a Shade." Behind all this sounds the ground-swell of his frustrated love for Maud Gonne. Because of a barren passion's sake he cannot offer his ancestors children to continue the family line, and yet his constant praise of her beauty and her love of the people whom he had begun to distrust continues; it spills over into poems published some years later in *The Wild Swans at Coole* (1919), such as "Her Praise," "His Phoenix," and "The People."

The Easter Rising of 1916 took Yeats by surprise. The revolutionaries he had come to despise attained heroic stature and it seemed to him that a terrible beauty was born. Maud Gonne's husband (from whom she had been separated) was one of the sixteen leaders executed, and Yeats went to France and proposed to her again, but, as in the past, she refused him. Then he asked her permission to propose to her adopted daughter Iseult,[1] to whom he had written several poems in preceding years. Iseult refused him, and in October 1917 he married Georgie Hyde-Lees whom he had known for some years. His marriage made his life "serene and full of order," and it also provided the starting-point for an altogether unexpected conjunction of his romantic and his realistic strains of poetry. Mrs. Yeats then attempted automatic writing because Yeats was unhappy at the beginning of their marriage (through concern over Iseult Gonne; later poems, "Two Songs of a Fool," "To a Young Beauty," "Michael Robartes and the Dancer" and "Owen Aherne and his Dancers," illustrate this), and to her surprise odd sentences were produced on a subject of which she knew nothing. Yeats was excited and stimulated, and spent hours every day on the decipherment of this automatic script; he seemed to be able to believe, even temporarily, in the system thus built up, which he published privately under the title of *A Vision* in 1925, and later, through Macmillan, in 1937.

This work is "a system of symbolism" (as Yeats explains in *A Packet for Ezra Pound,* 1934), which deals with various types of human personality, with the "gyres" of historical change and with the supernatural. It provided, in part, a structure for Yeats's thought, for the ideas he had been assimilating from his unusual reading. Its creation gave him confidence and strength so that he wrote out of all the fullness of his interests, finding in himself and his thought a sufficient subject for poetry. The first poems relating to *A Vision* appeared in *The Wild Swans at Coole* (1919), "The Phases of the Moon," and "Hic and Ille," and, perhaps the mos impressive of them, "The Second Coming" in *Michael Robartes and the Dancer* (1921). These two volumes show the reblossoming of his poetry after the cold winter rages of *Responsibilities.* In such poems as "In Memory of Major Robert Gregory," "Easter 1916," and "A Prayer for my Daughter," Yeats is able to write with authority, to blend his appreciation of beauty with a sense of the tragic rather than the pathetic elements of life, to give a significance to the ordinary events of life which his earlier poetry avoided, and to attain in the process a personal means of achieving public speech in poetry.

His life had blossomed too. The erstwhile revolutionary turned cynic now became a Senator of the Irish Free State, and an active constructive one at that; all the Senators, himself included, seemed to him like "coral insects with some design in our heads of

[1] Iseult was actually Maud Gonne's natural daughter. The father was a Frenchman named Millevoye.

the ultimate island." He spoke frequently and made his main contribution as Chairman of the Commission on Coinage (his Report is a model of its kind) though he regarded all matters connected with art or literature as coming within his province, and on these he was heard with respect. "Among School Children" gives us a brief vignette of him as a "sixty-year-old smiling public man."

The award of the Nobel Prize for poetry gave public recognition to his work. He had bought Thoor Ballylee, a Norman tower in Galway, where he now lived for part of the year. It was a visible symbol of the Anglo-Irish tradition which he began to explore excitedly. He read Swift, Goldsmith, Berkeley and Burke and saw himself as an inheritor of their traditions, where plain speech and clarity were the basis of rhetoric. The Yeats line was secure now, for the birth of his daughter was followed by that of a son. With this flowering of his life when the opposites seemed conjoined—poet and Nobel Prize winner, man of action and Senator—came the maturity of his style. He uses a symbolism which is direct speech, it records the richness of his life as well as its bitterness. As his youthful ambitions were realised he saw the paradoxes of life. Irish freedom was achieved, but the glorious great houses were burnt down. Wisdom might perhaps compensate him for the loss of youth; but as his body aged his muse grew younger, "the real man, the imagination which liveth for ever."[2] As a result he wrote "The Tower" and "Sailing to Byzantium," passionate poems of tension between the sensual and the spiritual, their unity arising out of his own complexity.

This warring of the antinomies continued in *The Winding Stair* (1933) in "A Dialogue of Self and Soul" with its triumphant pagan affirmation of belief in human life which was echoed later in "Vacillation." The contrast lay in the passing of glory. Coole Park, the significance of which as a focal point of Irish culture he celebrated in "Coole Park, 1929," had been sold to the Forestry Department of the Land Commission with the understanding that Lady Gregory should rent the house and part of the demesne until her death. Now in "Coole Park and Ballylee, 1931" he realises Lady Gregory is dying, and with her the dignity and loveliness of a house which symbolised the inherited yet living glory of an aristocratic life.

Yeats himself suffered from severe illness in the winter of 1927–28, as is evidenced by "At Algeciras—a Meditation upon Death," but the spring of 1929 was an exuberantly creative period

[2] Blake's phrase, quoted from what Yeats thought "the most beautiful" of Blake's letters.

when he wrote several of the Crazy Jane poems and the other lyrics which appeared in *Words for Music Perhaps* (1931).

A Full Moon in March (1935) contained Supernatural Songs, written out of a Donne-like delight in obscure thought condensed into arresting phrase. He was working with Shri Purohit Swami on a translation of the Upanishads and compiling *The Oxford Book of Modern Poetry* when he had another serious illness; but his poetry continued to develop and he prayed for "an old man's frenzy" in order to remake himself, to remodel his personality. He wrote out of rage and lust ("Why should not old men be mad?" asks one poem), but also out of a sense of simplicity and grandeur.[3] His moods of unity could produce in *Last Poems* such Olympian poetry as "The Municipal Gallery Revisited," or "Beautiful Lofty Things," in which he praised his friends generously and warmly, concentrating brilliantly upon aspects of their work or lives, which he caught in terse unforgettable phrases. "The Gyres" and "The Statues" reverted to the material of *A Vision,* while "The Circus Animals' Desertion" analysed his career with devastating honesty. Filled with energy, he fought death to the end, but in "The Man and the Echo" came to realise that all he knew was that he did not know what death brought. He hated old age; he called upon his ancestors to judge what he had done in "Are You Content?"; and he wrote "Under Ben Bulben" as his own epitaph and elegy, with all its passionate affirmation of what made up, for him, the indomitable qualities of the Irish, qualities which ensured the success of his long struggle to make himself a great and, always, an Irish poet. He died in Roquebrune in January 1939. His body was brought back to Ireland and interred at Drumcliff in September 1948.

[3] See *CP,* 299, 309, 333.

Frank Kermode

The Suffering Man, The Creative Mind

In the middle 'Thirties, emerging from my remote provincial background (but we wrote poems and asked whether Browning didn't sometimes go beyond bounds), I at last discovered Yeats and Eliot; and in that bewilderment one truth seemed worth steering by, which was that these men were *remaking* poetry. Although this recognition had very little to do with knowledge, and one waited years before being granted any real notion of the character of such poetry, it was nevertheless, as I still believe, a genuine insight. As one came to know the other great works of the wonderful years, one also came with increasing certainty to see that the imperative of modernism was "make it new": a difficult but in the end satisfactory formula.[1]

These were the years of Auden, of a poetry oscillating between an inaccessible private mythology and public exhortation, an in-group apocalypse and a call for commitment to "the struggle." It was going to be our war; we were committed whether or not we wanted to be; and there were many poems of Auden especially which have by now disappeared from the canon, but not from the memories of men in their forties. Meanwhile, as the war approached, the indisputably great, the men of the wonderful years, were still at work. What were they doing? Their commitment they consigned, mostly, to the cooler element of prose; but we could hardly suppose they were with any part of their minds on our side. "Making it new" seemed to be a process which

[1] The "imperative" is Ezra Pound's.

From "A Babylonish Dialect" in Continuities *by Frank Kermode. Copyright © 1968 by Frank Kermode. Reprinted by permission of Random House, Inc.*

had disagreeable consequences in the political sphere. I forget how we explained this to ourselves, but somehow we preserved the certainty that the older poets who behaved so strangely, seemed so harshly to absent themselves from our world—to hold in the age of the Bristol Bomber opinions which were appropriate to the penny-farthing—were nevertheless the men on whom all depended.

The death of Yeats in January, 1939, therefore seemed to us an event of catastrophic importance. The news of Eliot's death[2] immediately brought to mind, in surprising detail, the events and feelings of that dark, cold day nearly twenty-six years earlier. These were the men who had counted most, yet had seemed to have so little in common with us. Yet on the face of it the two events seemed to have little similarity beyond what is obvious. In the months preceding Yeat's death there had been an extraordinary outpouring of poetry—how impatiently one awaited the next issue of the *London Mercury,* and, later, the publication in the spring of 1940 of *Last Poems and Plays!* And that wasn't all: there was the poet himself, masked as a wild old man or a dangerous sage; there was the samurai posturing; the learned, more than half-fascist, shouting about eugenics and war, and this at a moment when we were beginning to understand that the enemy would soon be imposing both these disciplines on Europe. But one didn't hate the poet for what he thought he knew, remembering that he had always held strange opinions without damaging his verse. "Man can embody truth but he cannot know it," he said in his last letter; and years before, in a line which gives modern poetry its motto, "In dreams begin responsibilities." He made no order, but showed that our real lives begin when we have been shown that order ends: it is for the dreams, the intuitions of irregularity and chaos, of the tragic rag-and-bone shop, that we value him, and not for his "system" or his "thought." The time of his death seemed appropriate to the dream; in a few months the towns lay beaten flat.[3]

History did not collaborate in the same way to remind us of the responsibilities begun in Eliot's dream. His farewell to poetry was taken only a couple of years after Yeats's. It was no deathbed "Cuchulain Comforted"; it was "Little Gidding." Per-

[2] The essay from which this excerpt is taken was part of memorial issue of *The Sewanee Review* (Winter 1966) devoted to Eliot, who died in 1965.

[3] For the poems and prose referred to in this paragraph, see *On the Boiler; L,* 922; *CP,* 307, 97, 336, 292. (Kermode slightly misquotes the epigraph to *Responsibilities:* "In dreams begins responsibility.")

haps the Dantesque section of that poem grew in part from Yeats's strange poem; certainly Yeats predominates over the others who make up the "familiar compound ghost." The famous lines tell us what we ought to make of our great poetry and of our great poets:

> . . . 'I am not eager to rehearse
> My thought and theory which you have forgotten.
> These things have served their purpose: let them be.
> So with your own. . . .'

So much for the using up of a poet's thought. As a man he continues to suffer and without reward:

> 'Let me disclose the gifts reserved for age
> To set a crown upon your lifetime's effort.
> First, the cold friction of expiring sense. . . .
> Second, the conscious impotence of rage
> At human folly. . . .
> And last, the rending pain of re-enactment
> Of all that you have done, and been. . . .'

So the ghost speaks of a Yeatsian guilt, remorse, and purgation. The man who suffers is now truly distinct from the mind that creates poems that have to be, as Picasso said of paintings, "hordes of destructions."[4]

[4] "The more perfect the artist," Eliot said in 1917, "the more completely separate in him will be the man who suffers and the mind which creates" ("Tradition and the Individual Talent"). He spoke of a "second" (and greater) "impersonality" in his Yeats Memorial Lecture. See below, p. 28, n. .2

Patrick J. Keane

Embodied Song

I

All that is body, dancer; all that is spirit, bird.

Like his mentor William Blake, Yeats violated the usual pattern of romantic poets by creating wonderfully into his old age, his imagination growing, as Blake put it, "stronger & stronger as this Foolish Body decays."

> An aged man is but a paltry thing,
> A tattered coat upon a stick, unless
> Soul clap its hands and sing, and louder sing
> For every tatter in its mortal dress. (*CP,* 191)

Sing he did, man young and old; yet, that pivotal "unless" notwithstanding, "a raving autumn shears/Blossom from the summer's wreath" (*CP,* 229). We may "spit" into the transfiguring "face of Time," but decrepitude and "that discourtesy of death" will come (*CP,* 46, 131). And in any case, since "Love has pitched his mansion in/The place of excrement," soul is not enough. " 'Love is all/Unsatisfied/That cannot take the whole/Body and soul.'" That is "what Jane said" (*CP,* 255, 252), but much of Yeats's poetry is a variation on her text.

Faced with the inevitable ravaging of our mortal dress and of all that we value—"Old civilizations put to the sword"; "the ceremony of innocence. . .drowned" in the "blood-dimmed tide," the "darkening flood" of history; "Many ingenious lovely things . . .gone/That seemed sheer miracle to the multitude" (*CP,* 292, 184–85, 240, 204)—we must ask, as Yeats does in the last poem quoted ("Nineteen Hundred and Nineteen"),

> But is there any comfort to be found?
> Man is in love and loves what vanishes,
> What more is there to say? (*CP,* 205)

The more to say fills *Collected Poems,* with its "laughing, crying, sacred [,] . . . leching song" (*CP,* 295), its affirmation and denigration of life; astringent joy and anguished elegy; mingled gaiety and terror, assertion and despair, songs of both this world and the other, "sex and the dead" (*L,* 730). For Yeats had no final word. Only death could still that voice; and the comfort to be found lies, for example, in the fact that a seventy-three-year-old man could write, on his deathbed, so great a poem as "Cuchulain Comforted" (like the final fragments of Keats and Shelley, a testament haunted by Dante). The creation of a poem that places the poet's dead hero among his polar opposites in the other world, and is itself a triumph of the imagination on the edge of the abyss, is a profoundly moving embodiment of Yeats's centric myth: the interpenetration of gyring opposites, living each other's death, dying each other's life, "Lapis Lazuli's" "Black out; Heaven blazing into the head" (*CP,* 292). "I shall find the dark grow luminous, the void fruitful," Yeats wrote, "when I understand I have nothing, that the ringers in the tower have appointed for the hymen of the soul a passing bell" (*M,* 332).

In the meantime, as he says in this same section of *Per Amica Silentia Lunae,* "we sing amid our uncertainty," making "out of the quarrel with others, rhetoric, but of the quarrel with ourselves, poetry." Yeats's great quarrel with himself (though he sees it as the antagonism at the heart of the world as well) is that between what he calls the *"primary"* and the *"antithetical."* The *primary* or "objective" is "democratic," "that which serves," is directed "towards God" and "the soul's disappearance in God"; it is associated by Yeats with the self-denying Christian era, "levelling, unifying, feminine, humane, peace its means and end." The *antithetical* or "subjective" is "aristocratic," directed "towards Nature" and "the soul's ultimate, particular freedom"; it is associated by Yeats with the "polytheistic" pagan world of heroes and poets, when power, pride, passion, and conflict were "good," not "evil." "Hierarchical, masculine, harsh, surgical," this world is to be reborn in an *"antithetical* dispensation" which "must reverse our era," the gyre-reversing annunciations being dramatically incarnated in the poems "Leda and the Swan," "The Mother of God," and "The Second Coming."[1]

[1] In the scheme of *A Vision,* from which these definitions are taken (*V,* 85, 104, 52, 262–63), lunar phases 23 through 7 are predominantly *primary,* 9 through 21 predominantly *antithetical,* 8 and 22 being equal mixtures, while no human life is possible at 1 and 15, the dark and full moon respectively.

Though "very religious" (*A,* 77) and obsessed with the occult, Yeats seems predominantly *antithetical.* But his deepest commitment was to *conflict*—to the maintenance of tension between these warring impulses. "I am," he insisted in his 1930 diary, "always, in all I do, driven to a moment which is the realization of myself as unique and free, or to a moment which is the surrender to God of all that I am. . . .Surely if either circuit, that which carries us into man or that which carries us into God, were reality, the generation had long since found its term" (*Ex,* 305, 307). In one of his most explicit, most dramatic (and, incidentally, most Nietzschean) lines, Yeats declares: "Homer is my example and his unchristened heart." But the poem in which the line occurs is entitled "Vacillation"; it begins, "Between extremities/Man runs his course," and ends, "So get you gone, Von Hügel, though with blessings on your head" (*CP,* 245, 247). For Yeats, though he affirms the position of the *antithetical* Heart, admits that he and the Catholic mystic Von Hügel share a belief in miracles, and the parting from him seems genuinely reluctant, far (though there is a patronizing tone as well) from the brusque dismissal he would receive at the hands of what Yeats called the "machine-shop" realist.

Between these extremities, therefore, Yeats continues to run his vacillating course, the resultant tension generating—and this is the essential, defining element of his poetry—*power.* Transforming abstract polarities into concrete *personae* representing this battle (Self or Homeric Heart vs. Platonic-Christian Soul, Oisin vs. St. Patrick, Crazy Jane vs. the Bishop, etc.), Yeats indeed made, out of the lifelong quarrel with himself, poetry. But if prevalence of either "circuit" or their premature reconciliation were two dangers to be avoided, mere vacillation was a third and, it would seem, poetically the most perilous. If, to employ Yeats's most-quoted lines, "the best lack all conviction, while the worst/ Are full of passionate intensity" (*CP,* 185), then one must go beyond such categories, so that, while avoiding dogmatic "convictions," one may speak, through a variety of "masks," with "passionate intensity." Avoiding mere wavering indecision, Yeats affirms one position, then the other, in a continuing series of projections of his internal dialogue. Dramatically exploiting his vacillation, he made sure that emphasis fell on the song rather than the uncertainty, attaining what Ellmann calls "affirmative capability" in the face of personal skepticism, "assertion without doctrine."

The great debate between Heart and Soul in "Vacillation" "puts clearly an argument that has gone on in my head for years,"

Yeats wrote Olivia Shakespear (*L,* 789). We are dealing, then, not only with the major stimulus and source of power in the poetry, but with a genuine and apparently inexhaustible source. No romantic comet, Yeats dominated the firmament of English poetry for half a century—from *The Wanderings of Oisin,* published in 1889, until that "dark cold day" in January 1939 when, in W. H. Auden's words of elegy, "he became his admirers." And very nearly "all the instruments agree" on his continued preeminence among modern poets—for some critics, the greatest since Milton; even the greatest *lyric* poet in the language.

A handful of critics—most recently and most formidably, Conor Cruise O'Brien and Harold Bloom—have accepted Yeats's invitation to "Come, fix upon me that accusing eye" (*CP,* 275). They have revealed some defects in the work, some warts concealed by the received portrait of the man. That is to be expected, even desired, in the case of a man and poet who was perhaps becoming rather too solidly established as the subject of idolatry. But, like the lunar visage that transcends both stain and "Odour of blood on the ancestral stair," the final image of Yeats will survive all attacks and revisionism. His "true self, my poems" (*Ex,* 308) ensure that: "for no stain/Can come upon the visage of the moon/ When it has looked in glory from a cloud" (*CP,* 234).

II

"My true self, my poems." *Man and Poet; The Man and the Masks:* subtitles of critical biographies of Yeats. Much has been written about the complex interaction between Yeats's life and work. His own prose made this inevitable. Indeed, Yeats valued "personality" ("delight in the whole man—blood, imagination, intellect, running together" [*E&I,* 266]); thought he would be a great poet if he were granted an exciting life and noble friends; and took extraordinary care that his own life and the lives of those friends, as well as his "ideas," were made sufficiently public to illuminate the poetry. "I have no sympathy with the . . . thought . . . that a poet's life concerns nobody but himself," he observed in a 1910 lecture entitled "Friends of my Youth."

> A poet is by the very nature of things a man who lives with entire sincerity, or rather the better his poetry the more sincere his life; his life is an experiment in living and those that come after him have a right to know it. Above all it is necessary that the lyric poet's life

> should be known that we should understand that his poetry is no rootless flower but the speech of a man.

"Entire sincerity" points toward Yeats's ideal "Unity of Being"; "experiment" toward his search for the proper "mask." The goals seem contradictory, but it is through the latter, Yeats insists, that the former is attained. But what *is* the connection between flower and speech, between the poetry and the man who made it?

There are of course differences between what the man is and what he sings. The "mask" is, in fact, his opposite; the figure "most unlike, being my anti-self" (*CP,* 159). Take, again, the central embodiment of the Yeatsian heroic mask. Representing "creative joy separated from fear" (*L,* 913), Cuchulain is gay and reckless; dancer, warrior, cherisher of folly. His is the "hand that loves to scatter; the life like a gambler's throw," praised in *The Green Helmet* (*CPl,* 159). Choosing his tragic fate, shouldering the spear and asserting his identity at the conclusion of *At the Hawk's Well,* he strikes the true heroic note of impersonal self-recognition: "He comes! Cuchulain, son of Sualtim, comes!" (*CPl,* 144) Though readers have been discomfited by the end Yeats reserves for his hero (no longer "Cuchulain, son of Sualtim," but a nameless "man" placed among his *primary* opposites, "convicted cowards all"), "Cuchulain Comforted" nevertheless seems a myth-determined and very personal reconciliation of opposites. The hero had described his momentary vision in *The Death of Cuchulain:*

> There floats out there
> The shape that I shall take when I am dead,
> My soul's first shape, a soft feathery shape,
> And is not that a strange shape for the soul
> Of a great fighting-man? (*CPl,* 444)

The hero may be perplexed; not so his creator—who had earlier imagined *his* soul taking the *hard* shape of a metallic bird,, knowing himself to be one with a "timid heart" who only "ruffled in a manly pose" (*CP,* 238). Yeats, in short, identified with Cuchulain without confusing himself with him. Had he been a Cuchulain, or even the successful lover of Maud Gonne, he "might have thrown poor words away/ And been content to live" (*CP,* 89). He was neither, and created out of his inadequacies; for, as Yeats had read in a book he was studying during the composition of the first Cuchulain play, "Homer would not have created an Achilles nor Goethe a Faust if Homer had been an Achilles or Goethe a Faust" (Nietzsche, *On the Genealogy of Morals*).

Yeats the Poet consistently celebrated that "life like a gambler's throw," the "wasteful virtues [that] earn the sun," the heroes who, with Castiglionian *sprezzatura,* "weighed so lightly what they gave," and "gave, though free to refuse" (*CP,* 99, 107, 196). The Irish airman shot down in the Great War is motivated by nothing conventionally explicable, nothing external to himself:

> Nor law, nor duty bade me fight,
> Nor public men, nor cheering crowds,
> A lonely impulse of delight
> Drove to this tumult in the clouds. . . . (*CP,* 133)

Similarly, conventional limitations—moral "bans" (*CP,* 266); the thought control of censorship; the timidities and vulgarities of that "baptism of the gutter," democracy; the money-grubbing of middle-class Paudeens, "born to pray and save" and "fumble in a greasy till" (*CP,* 106); the reductive mills of logic and mere rationalism—are the objects of aristocratic contempt. The conscious precursors (neatly fused by Yeats to serve his own purposes) are Blake, for whom "Prudence is a rich ugly old maid courted by Incapacity," and Nietzsche, with his *"gaya scienza,"* and advice to "*live dangerously!* Build your cities under Vesuvius! Send your ships into uncharted seas!" The "morality" of "Art," Yeats wrote, "is personal, knows little of any general law, . . . seems lighter than a breath and yet is hard and heavy, for a man must be ready to face risk and toil, and in all gaiety of heart. . . ." And he rails against democratic-Christian "hatred of all that was abundant, extravagant, exuberant, of all that sets a sail for shipwreck. . . ." (*E&I,* 292–93, 105).

Yeats the Man, however, tended to practice other than the Poet preached, sounding like Shakespeare's Mark Antony, acting like "Caesar Augustus that made all the laws/ And the ordering of everything" (in a draft version of stanza 6 of "Among School Children"). Yeats planned his life with the Roman calculation of a man who, despite the insistence of his "Tom O'Roughley" that "An aimless joy is a pure joy," "has marked a distant object down" (*CP,* 139). He was perfectly willing to "seem/ For the song's sake a fool" (*CP,* 281), but Yeats, as Conor Cruise O'Brien has observed, was not the "foolish, passionate man" of "A Prayer for Old Age," but "something much more interesting: a cunning passionate man"; or, at least, a man who balanced against Blake's, Edmund

Burke's attitude toward prudence. Unwilling, perhaps, to betray his "tragic generation," Yeats experimented with hashish and—in 1898, under the supervision of Havelock Ellis—with mescaline. But he preferred to cleanse the doors of perception, not chemically, but alchemically, through imagination. And, for Yeats, imagination required intellect; energy, order. He might mock those "practical men who believe in money, in position, in a marriage bell" (*M*, 331), but he wrote this soon after his own marriage and all three items are among the catalogue of accomplishments given (with saving irony) in the late poem "What Then?"

The two sides of the Yeatsian penny, the practical objective and the imaginative subjective, are dramatized in such confrontations as those between Conchubar and Cuchulain, Owen Aherne and Michael Robartes. The poet's heart (in both the common and Yeatsian senses) is clearly enough with Cuchulain and Robartes; but, just as Blake, while making his own "preference" unmistakable, insists on the necessity for *both* "Reason" and "Energy" (Urizen and Orc); and just as Nietzsche emphasizes the maintenance of a fruitful *agon* between the Apollonian and the Dionysian, so Yeats realized the need for both sides of his antithesis. For example: ideally, "wisdom" is not laboriously extracted "out of midnight oil" (*CP,* 214), but in our sublunary world, the fallen world of "Adam's Curse," seeming spontaneity is actually the result of "discipline" and "bloody press" (*CPl,* 185), calculated artifice which the artifact, the poem, must then conceal:

> A line will take us hours maybe;
> Yet if it does not seem a moment's thought,
> Our stitching and unstitching has been naught. (*CP,* 78)

In what he called, in "The Statues," "these/ Calculations that seem but casual flesh" (*CP,* 322); or here, in the certainty that "there is no fine thing/ Since Adam's fall but needs much labouring," we have the interaction, and the distinction, between work and "the work of art," between the laboring man who must strain and sweat and the *seeming* nonchalance and iconic harmony of that "Labour [which] is blossoming or dancing where/ The body is not bruised to pleasure soul" (*CP,* 214).

Frequently, Yeats implies that the artist, Homerically preoccupied with sin and *this* world, bruises soul to pleasure body and imagination, and at such times, as in "The Choice," the dichotomy between the life and the work becomes fundamental, even fundamentalist:

> The intellect of man is forced to choose
> Perfection of the life or of the work,
> And if it take the second must refuse
> A heavenly mansion, raging in the dark. (*CP*, 242)

Then the line blurs again, as in Yeats's last letter: "'Man can embody truth but he cannot know it.' I must embody it in the completion of my life" (*L*, 922). In this sense, the life itself is the total work of art, the completed symbol; and we are reminded of Yeats's insistence that "style" is the writer's form of "self-conquest"; that "Whenever I remake a song/ . . . It is myself that I remake" (*A*, 349; *VP*, 778). And yet, pointing back as it does to the language of "The Choice," the ironically autobiographical "What Then?" makes it clear that the "Something to perfection brought" (*CP*, 300) is the work, and only that. Indeed, the mounting derision of "Plato's ghost" implies that the price of the poet's devotion to his art may be forfeiture of eternal life—that "heavenly mansion" forsworn first in "The Choice" and later by Crazy Jane (*CP*, 242, 254).

But the ruins of time build other—aesthetic—mansions in eternity. In the end, we are faced with *Collected Poems* and *Collected Plays*, a composite "sacred book of the arts" wrung from the profanities and ignominy of personal human experience, mire and blood transmuted to Byzantine gold. The poetry is, indeed, "no rootless flower but the speech of a man"—as the old woman says of the body of Adonis in "Her Vision in the Wood," "no fabulous symbol there/ But my heart's victim and its torturer" (*CP*, 243, 270). It is a "great-rooted blossomer" sprung from a variety of fecund ditches, not a Christian but a Homeric "pattern on a napkin dipped in blood," a divine birth "not from a void"—the "empty tomb or virgin womb" of the Blakean and blasphemous "A Stick of Incence"—but "of our own rich experience" (*CP*, 214, 235, 329; *Ex*, 436–37). For "Only an aching heart/ Conceives a changeless work of art" (*CP*, 200).

"A poet writes always out of his personal life," Yeats admitted, "in his finest work out of its tragedy, whatever it be, remorse, lost love, or mere loneliness." But the "First Principle" of his *art* was that "even when the poet seems most himself, [he] is never the bundle of accident that sits down to breakfast; he has been reborn as an idea, something intended, complete . . . more type than man, more passion than type" (*E&I*, 509). This distancing and partial impersonalizing of private emotion through art—so salient a feature of Yeats's poetic revisions—involves both a rejection of the Eliotic escape from personality and an anticipatory rejection of our more extreme "confessional" poetry.[2] For all that is merely personal "soon rots; it must be packed in ice or salt," and "ancient salt is best packing" (*E&I,* 522). Hencc Yeats's emphasis on "a traditional stanza" (like his own favorite, *ottava rima*); his realization that, in Aristotelian terminology, the artist is only the poem's efficient cause; that it has form and therefore a formal cause, which can only be attained through constant "remaking." Pursuing this distinction, Northrop Frye has written: "The poet's task is to deliver the poem in as uninjured a state as possible, and if the poem is alive, it is equally anxious to be rid of him, and screams to be cut loose from his private memories and associations, his desire for self-expression, and all the other navel-strings and feeding tubes of his ego" ("The Archetypes of Literature"). Yeats is never quite *that* surgical, but surely the private navel-strings clinging to his poems are less important than that "navelcord," the "strandentwining cable of all flesh" *(Ulysses),* umbilically linking us all to the human condition, and so back to Stephen Dedalus's "Edenville," and to that *Anima Mundi* or archetypal storehouse from which Yeats draws his own particular stock of images.

All of which is to say that we are concerned, as usual when dealing with Yeats, with a double movement. The first is from private emotion, "the foul rag-and-bone shop of the heart," to "masterful images" and symbolic patterns; the second, from pattern to dramatic embodiment in specific poems and plays: the perpetual return to the starting point in the rag-and-bone shop, but with the emotion distanced and objectified in an art characterized by protective symbols which finally enlist their own allegiances. *The Wanderings of Oisin,* Yeats admitted, embodied personal, cryptic "themes of the embittered heart." The same was true, he continued in the poem from which I've been quoting ("The Circus

[2] In early essays, particularly "Tradition and the Individual Talent," Eliot extolled impersonality. It is significant that later, in his Memorial Lecture on Yeats, he distinguished "two forms of impersonality," connecting Yeats with the second and greater form: that of the poet who, "out of intense and personal experience, is able to express a general truth; retaining all the particularity of his experience, to make of it a general symbol." Eliot seems to echo Yeats's own comment that he wove "an always personal emotion. . .into a general pattern of myth and symbol" (*A,* 101–2).

As for the anticipatory rejection of "confessional" poetry: after "reading poems by certain young writers in an American magazine of verse" in 1930, Yeats jotted in his diary: "The heart well worn upon the sleeve may be the best of sights,/ But never, never dangling leave the liver and the lights" (*Ex,* 291).

Animals' Desertion"), of his early play *The Countess Cathleen,* written for Maud Gonne, and *On Baile's Strand,* the first of the Cuchulain plays:

> Heart-mysteries there, and yet when all is said
> It was the dream itself enchanted me:
> Character isolated by a deed
> To engross the present and dominate memory.
> Players and painted stage took all my love,
> And not those things that they were emblems of. (*CP,* 336)

Yeats, the Man and the Poet, the Man and the Masks, the Identity: ultimately, the life and work *do* form, if not that unity Yeats sought all his life, a complex interdependence. For the poems, even the "Maud Gonne" poems, are never *mere* autobiography. As M. L. Rosenthal has said of "No Second Troy," "although Yeats used real experience for the dramatic situation of the poem he was guided as well by conceptions and symbolic associations not necessarily dependent on that experience. . . ." And, in the end, the final—"complete"—integrity inheres only in such symbols, in such "masterful images" as those which rapturously transcend the problems of the divided self dramatized in the earlier stanzas of "Among School Children":

> O chestnut-tree, great-rooted blossomer,
> Are you the leaf, the blossom, or the bole?
> O body swayed to music, O brightening glance,
> How can we know the dancer from the dance? (*CP,* 214)

III

Great images and epiphanic "moments" reconcile antinomies; but such reconciliations are permanent only "There," in the land of heart's desire beyond the world of mere Becoming, Blake's "vegetable glass of nature." We are "Here," in that vegetable world, dancing figures "caught in that sensual music" (*CP,* 191). In Platonic (or Socratic-Christian) moods, Yeats thought it absurd that we cannot bring the flesh to heel; and on such occasions it seemed time he "made" his "soul," time to board the ship of death, sailing out of Nature into Perfection, "the holy city of Byzantium." The world of generation is then perceived as "no country for old men"—old men who "must bid the Muse go pack,/ Choose Plato and Plotinus for a friend"; or turn their attention to "monuments of unageing intellect," Byzantine gold and mosaic, "the proud stones of Greece," "beauty that is cast out of a mould/ In bronze, or that in dazzling marble appears." And all this because, "The living beauty is for younger men;/ We cannot pay its tribute of wild tears" (*CP,* 191, 197, 192, 196, 137).

But, as he noted with astonishment in his late sixties, his poetry constituted one long protest against old age and death, and the wisdom that comes with age was never convincingly accepted as the "abundant recompense" of the more resigned Wordsworth—not even in the final lines of "The Tower" (a poem that began, incidentally, with oblique mockery of Wordsworth's dotage):

> Now shall I make my soul,
> Compelling it to study
> In a learned school
> Till the wreck of body,
> Slow decay of blood,
> Testy delirium,
> Or what worse evil come—
> The death of friends, or death
> Of every brilliant eye
> That made a catch in the breath—
> Seem but the clouds of the sky
> When the horizon fades,
> Or a bird's sleepy cry
> Among the deepening shades. (*CP,* 197)

This is majestic, but the softer *Oisin* music that haunts its rhetoric cannot dissolve the felt pain of bodily decay and death. The compulsory lesson, after the manner of its kind, never fully takes. The tribute of tears continues to be paid; the anguish and radical frustration of the human predicament remain: "Bodily decrepitude is wisdom; young/ We loved each other and were ignorant" (*CP,* 260). It is significant that Yeats intended *Collected Poems* to conclude, not with the uneven and pontifical voice from beyond the grave of "Under Ben Bulben," but with the little poem whose final lines recapture the piercing cry of the old lyric ("Christ, if my love were in my armes,/ And I in my bed againe"): "But O that I were young again/ And held her in my arms!" (*CP,* 337). Poet rather than Saint, Yeats admitted in his late sixties, "I shall be a sinful man to the end, and think upon my death-bed of all the nights I wasted in my youth" (*L,* 790).

Behind all such cries stands, ultimately, the imposing figure of Maud Gonne—the beautiful Irish revolutionary who was Yeats's cruel but magnificent Helen ("Why, what could she have done, being what she is?/ Was there another Troy for her to burn?"), the "woman lost" upon whom the poet's "imagination dwells the most" (*CP,* 89, 195). "If there were no Maud Gonne Yeats would have invented her." Perhaps; but there *was* a Maud Gonne and there is no reason to doubt that Yeats loved her deeply and that he suffered.

"I was twenty-three years old when the troubling of my life began." His "devotion," he said, "might as well have been offered to an image in a milliner's window, or to a statue in a museum" (*A,* 267). Her own beauty and character, poetically embellished, made her a living fusion of Helen, Beatrice, Laura, the romantic *femme fatale,* the pre-Raphaelite "stunner," an ancient Irish queen, Ireland herself. He strove to love her "in the old high way of love" (*CP,* 79)—in vain. Repeatedly, over a period of a quarter-century, before her marriage to John MacBride and after MacBride's execution by the British, Yeats asked her to marry him. Because "you make beautiful poetry out of what you call your unhappiness," Maud told him, "the world should thank me for not marrying you" (*A Servant of the Queen,* p. 329). He admits as much himself in the poem "Words" (*CP,* 88), and his readers have ever since offered up a mixed tribute of gratitude and "blame."

Occupying the point at which the poet's life and work most dramatically converge, Maud Gonne becomes more than the remarkable woman bound by the dates 1866–1953, and more than another *domina* or *belle dame sans merci* in the Renaissance and romantic traditions. She becomes, I think, an incarnation of that morality of Art which, according to Yeats, "is hard and heavy," but which must be faced "in all gaiety of heart"; in what he calls in "The Gyres" and "Lapis Lazuli" "tragic joy" and dread-transfiguring "gaiety" (*CP,* 291, 292). Her aesthetic "justification," in short, is in the painful "ecstasy" she evoked, an ecstasy which a great poet transformed into great art.

All those songs "Rhymed out in love's despair/ To flatter beauty's ignorant ear" (*CP,* 139), those poems of "a man/ Lying alone on a bed/ Remembering a woman's beauty" (*CPl,* 262), are the children of an unconsummated, or, at least, unrequited love. Denied "life," Yeats fell back upon "poor words," leaving in the glass of his poetry an imperishable shadow of that "arrogant loveliness," that "form all full/ As though with magnanimity of light," that "Ledaean body" (*CP,* 88, 176, 328, 213). "A woman Homer sung," Yeats's Helen was born out of phase, her noble, heroic, violent beauty "not natural in an age like this."[3] Consequently, though "the loveliest woman born," she traded the cornucopia of life "for an old bellows full of angry wind," the fanatical streetcorner screaming of "a Helen of social welfare dream" (*CP,* 187, 333). Whatever we may think of Yeats's politics and attitude toward women activists, we are forced to listen when he tells us, in the late poem "A Bronze Head," that "even at the starting post" he had perceived the wildness in her," the "vision of terror" he felt must shatter her soul, and had himself "grown wild/ And wandered murmuring everywhere, 'My child, my child!'" (*CP,* 329).

That is the cry of pain, and pain far removed from attitudinizing self-pity; the cry of a man lifted by the experience of a long life beyond his own roots among the nineties' fastidious amateurs of grief. Rooted in the anguish of a crossed love, poor words became the vehicle of "vision, . . . the revelation of reality—ecstasy," for ecstasy "cannot exist without pain." "He only," Yeats continues in this passage in *Per Amica Silentia Lunae,* "can create the greatest imaginable beauty who has endured the greatest imaginable pangs" (*M,* 331). As the cause of so much suffering, Maud must be not merely accepted ("the lot of love is chosen," actively, heroically) but affirmed "again/ And yet again" (*CP,* 268, 232). Yeats concludes "Friends," his poem of "praise" and gratitude to those "Three women that have wrought/ What joy is in my days," by turning from Olivia Shakespear and Lady Gregory to "her that took/ All till my youth was gone/ With scarce a pitying look." "How could I praise that one?" he asks, answering as only Yeats could answer:

> When day begins to break
> I count my good and bad,
> Being wakeful for her sake,
> Remembering what she had,
> What eagle look still shows,
> While up from my heart's root
> So great a sweetness flows
> I shake from head to foot. (*CP,* 122)

That sweetness flows again in the ecstatic peroration of what may be Yeats's central poem, "A Dialogue of Self and Soul." For

[3] *CP,* 87, 89. This is a recurrent theme. As Ellmann says of this poem ("No Second Troy"), "the poet attacks the Troy-less present for not being heroically inflammable" (*Identity,* p. 112). Cf. The conclusions of "The Statues," "A Bronze Head," and "Coole Park and Ballylee, 1931."

the affirmation of the most painful experience of his life—that "love crossed long ago" (*CP,* 123)—leads to an affirmation of *all* existence. The summoning Soul's imperious offer of "ancestral night that can,/ If but imagination scorn the earth/. . . Deliver from the crime of death and birth" is rejected in favor of "Heart's purple," and the Self's heroic choice "to live it all again/ And yet again," omitting no toil, ignominy, pain; including, above all, "that most fecund ditch of all,/ The folly that man does/ Or must suffer, if he woos/ A proud woman not kindred of his soul." The recovery of what Yeats elsewhere calls the soul's self-delighting, self-appeasing "radical innocence" (*CP,* 187) is attained in the final stanza:

> I am content to follow to its source
> Every event in action or in thought;
> Measure the lot; forgive myself the lot!
> When such as I cast out remorse
> So great a sweetness flows into the breast
> We must laugh and we must sing,
> We are blest by everything,
> Everything we look upon is blest. (*CP,* 232)

Though the voice of Self, in its creative joy and the sweetness of its exaltation, is unmistakably that of Yeats, its blending of, among others, the voices of Blake and Nietzsche may be confirmed by Yeats himself. In his *Autobiography,* after slightly misquoting Blake's "praise of life—'all that lives is holy,'" he immediately adds, "Nietzsche had it doubtless at the moment when he imagined the 'Superman' as a child."[4] "The child is innocence and forgetting," says Nietzsche's Zarathustra, "a new beginning, a game, a self-propelled wheel, . . . a sacred 'Yes!'" In this poem, his "choice of rebirth rather than deliverance from birth" (*L,* 729), Yeats captures not only this "sacred 'Yes,'" but both Zarathustra's exhortation to *"remain faithful to the earth,"* and his song ("Once More!") to eternity, sung after he has whispered into the ear of Life the secret that he shall die and recur: "Deep is [the world's] woe;/ Joy—deeper yet than agony:/ Woe implores: Go!/ But all joy wants eternity—/ Wants deep, wants deep eternity!" For anyone who feels, as I do, that "Dialogue" is Yeats's conscious version of Nietzsche's linked doctrines of *amor fati* and Eternal Recurrence,

[4] *A,* 321. Yeats consistently linked the two, believing that "Nietzsche completes Blake and has the same roots," and that Nietzschean thought "flows always, though with an even more violent current, in the bed Blake's thought has worn" (*L,* 379; *E&I,* 130).

the best parallel *is* Zarathustra: who jumps "with both feet" into "golden-emerald delight," and into a cluster of images and motifs we would call—Yeatsian:

> In laughter all that is evil comes together, but is pronounced holy and absolved by its own bliss; and if this is my alpha and omega, that all that is heavy and grave should become light; all that is body, dancer; all that is spirit, bird—and verily, that is my alpha and omega: Oh, how should I not lust after eternity and the nuptial ring of rings, the ring of recurrence?[5]

Whether or not it is a consciously Nietzschean-Dionysian affirmation of existence in all its tangled totality of joy and pain, "A Dialogue of Self and Soul" remains but half the story—the lifeward-turning answer of *The Winding Stair* to "Sailing to Byzantium" in the deathward-turning volume, *The Tower.* But when Self claims "a charter to commit the crime once more" it *is* a repudiation of the previous petition to the "singing-masters of my soul" to "consume my heart away," to sweep the "dying animal" "out of nature . . . into the artifice of eternity" (*CP,* 231, 191–92). The powerful impulse of Soul—which drew Yeats to Tir-na-nOg, to Byzantium, to Indian holy mountains, as concrete projections of *A Vision's* Sphere or final resting place—was countered by the still more powerful, *antithetical* pull of Self toward passionate life and the antinomies. However drawn toward Being, Yeats either makes his paradises human (like Pound in the *Cantos*) or implies their inherent limitation: precisely that which makes them permanent also makes them cold and inhuman—a central theme from "The Stolen Child" (1886) on. Thus, even in the overtly *primary* or soul-directed Byzantium poems, the *antithetical* or life-directed impulse is too passionate to be programmatically subdued. We remember (as with Keats's odes) the rich plenitude of the sexual world being "rejected" in the first poem; the ambiguity of the famous phrase, "the *artifice* of eternity"; the power of "Byzantium's" final "images that yet/ Fresh images beget,/ That dolphin-torn, that gong-tormented sea" (*CP,* 191, 244). In this last case, we almost forget that the goldsmiths and marbles are said to "break" these spawning images, these "furies of complexity." ("The governing force of the verb 'break,'" as Helen Vendler has remarked, "is spent long before the end of the stanza is reached,

[5] Nietzsche quotations in this paragraph are taken from Walter Kaufmann's translation of *Thus Spoke Zarathustra,* part I, prologue and section 1; III.15 (cf.IV.19); III.16.

and the last three lines stand syntactically as absolutes.") Yeats, unleashing the power of the *antithetical,* leaves us, as usual, dynamically suspended at the point of intersection of his two worlds.

IV

Attracted to, and repelled by, the "other" world, the austere way of the Soul; unable to surrender even what he has forsworn, Yeats remains, like all of us, "caught between the pull/ Of the dark moon and the full" (*CP,* 169). The mystical ideal has never been more starkly expressed than by St. John of the Cross: "The soul cannot be possessed of the divine union until it has divested itself of the love of created beings." Here, as elsewhere, the contrast is notable between Yeats and Eliot, who employed this statement as an epigraph to *Sweeney Agonistes.* Challenged by a friend who "regarded this with horror," Eliot replied that "for people seriously engaged in pursuing the Way of Contemplation," and "read in relation to that Way, . . . the doctrine is fundamentally true."[6]

For Yeats, on the other hand, the Way of St. John (and of Eliot) was the most degenerate form of the *primary* "objective" tendency. "What is this God," he asked in a canceled note to his play *Calvary,* "for whom He [Christ] taught the saints to lacerate their bodies, to starve and exterminate themselves, but the spiritual objective?"[7] This was a "sanctity of the cell and of the scourge," and

> since the Renaissance the writing of the European saints . . . has ceased to hold our attention. We know that we must at last forsake the world, and we are accustomed in moments of weariness or exaltation to consider a voluntary forsaking; but how can we, who have read so much poetry, seen so many paintings, listened to so much music, where the cry of the flesh and the cry of the soul seem one, forsake it harshly and rudely? What have we in common with St. Bernard covering his eyes that they may not dwell upon the beauty of the lakes of Switzerland . . . ? (*E&I,* 392–93)

"Where the cry of the flesh and the cry of the soul seem one"; for "Labour is blossoming or dancing where/ The body is not bruised to pleasure soul" (*CP,* 214).

[6] Bonamy Dobrée, "T. S. Eliot: A Personal Reminiscence," in *T. S. Eliot: The Man and His Work,* ed. Allen Tate, Delta Books, New York, 1966, p. 81.

[7] Quoted in F. A. C. Wilson, *Yeats's Iconography,* p. 323, n. 41.

Hungry for Unity and suspended between the realms he would unify, Yeats appears to conclude that the world of nature and the world of spirit are interdependent aspects of an underlying "reality" which manifests itself—provisionally, "Here"—in the form of contrast, polarity, the antinomies. That ultimate reality he can apprehend only in isolated moments; the more dynamic, and dramatic, interdependence becomes his major motif. Being is seen as rooted in Becoming, pure images as fueled by "the unpurged images of day" which "recede" but are never fully obliterated in the simplifying fire: for "'Whatever flames upon the night/ Man's own resinous heart has fed"; and, in the play which this song concludes, *The Resurrection,* Yeats places a beating Dionysian heart in the phantom bosom of Christ. Similarly, when the poet's Platonic "ladder's gone," he too, as we have seen, "must lie down where all the ladders start,/ In the foul rag-and-bone shop of the heart" (*CP,* 243, 211, 336; *CPl,* 373).

The proper country for old men or not, the world of "blood," of "those dying generations," of "Heart's purple," of "Poet's imaginings/ And memories of love" (*CP,* 191, 231, 234, 196) cannot be denied. Perhaps Yeats's complex of attitudes is most succinctly summarized in his rendering of the chorus from *Antigone,* the conclusion of his sequence *A Woman Young and Old:*

> Pray I will and sing I must,
> And yet I weep—Oedipus' child
> Descends into the loveless dust. (*CP,* 272)

Yeats, who rarely breaks up his own lines to weep, follows Sophocles here, but, echoing "A Dialogue of Self and Soul," sings in addition to praying and weeping. Bittersweet song and tragic joy for this life, prayer for the next. "And yet I weep." In the end, we really have no choice about paying the living, and dying, beauty (in this poem, "the soft cheek of a girl") its "tribute of wild tears."

It is when Yeats's song is mixed with something close to tears that, I think, we come closest to him. There is little danger of sentimentality—that "prevailing decadence . . . got under foot in my own heart" (*L,* 432) as early as 1904. And, like honey flowing from the mouth of strength—"The lion and the honeycomb, what has Scripture said?" (*CP,* 247)—softness and tears are dramatic in a man only when that man has deliberately cultivated "hardness" and "a cold eye." It is touching, but in no way sentimental, that Yeats should end his haunting death-poem "The Man and the

Echo" with the greatest of his many open questions and with his thought interrupted by the deathcry of the very animal employed at the start of his poetic career (in part 1 of *The Wanderings of Oisin*) as a symbol of mortality.

> O Rocky Voice,
> Shall we in that great night rejoice?
> What do we know but that we face
> One another in this place?
> But hush, for I have lost the theme,
> Its joy or night seem but a dream;
> Up there some hawk or owl has struck,
> Dropping out of sky or rock,
> A stricken rabbit is crying out,
> And its cry distracts my thought. (*CP,* 338–39)

In this, one of Yeats's great moments, the supernatural "joy or night" waiting beyond the grave dissolve in the poet's—the *man's*—sudden refocusing upon the violence and anguish of life itself. The thought of the unmasked old man is now distracted, not by the predatory birds associated with war (*V,* 27–28) and with Cuchulain (the son of "that clean hawk out of the air" [*CPl,* 168]), but by a stricken, *"primary"* animal. The putting aside of the heroic mask—like the earlier casting off of the "coat/ Covered with embroideries/ Out of old mythologies," and the more recent circus animals' desertion—implies no repudiation. Iconic coat, animals, and mask have performed their function and, "all work done," their creator at last descends, "naked," into his own "timid heart" (*CP,* 125, 338, 238). Samurai posturing and facile heroics pale before this genuine, self-confronting courage. "Why," Yeats had asked almost three decades earlier, "Why should we honor those who die upon the field of battle, a man may show as reckless a courage in entering into the abyss of himself" (quoted in Ellman, *Yeats: The Man and the Masks,* p. 6).

And this, it seems to me, is how we ought to read the poem praised at the outset of these remarks. "Cuchulain Comforted" strikes us with such authority precisely because Yeats leaves his hero not only in a *primary* condition, but in the *primary* condition least attractive to him personally—no blood-tingling surrender to a master-god, as in "Leda and the Swan" (*CP,* 211), but, rather, absorption into a discarnate, communal sewing bee that seems a strange parody of the "vast design" woven by the artisans of Yeats's Unified Culture. It is a visionary deathbed reconciliation of "All those antinomies/ Of day and night" (*CP,* 245), of "swordsman" and "saint" (*L,* 798), hero and poet, recklessness and cowardice, "creative joy" and "fear" (*L,* 913), song and uncertainty, the *antithetical* heroic mask and his own timid heart in hiding; as well as a final metamorphosis of the bird of Byzantium "set upon a golden bough to sing," that "bird's sleepy cry/ Among the deepening shades," and Nietzsche's "spirit" become "bird." With it we may well let Yeats "Float out upon a long/ Last reach of glittering stream/ And there sing his last song" (*CP,* 196).

A man that had six mortal wounds, a man
Violent and famous, strode among the dead;
Eyes stared out of the branches and were gone.

Then certain Shrouds that muttered head to head
Came and were gone. He leant upon a tree
As though to meditate on wounds and blood.

A Shroud that seemed to have authority
Among those bird-like things came, and let fall
A bundle of linen. Shrouds by two and three

Came creeping up because the man was still.
And thereupon that linen-carrier said:
'Your life can grow much sweeter if you will

'Obey our ancient rule and make a shroud;
Mainly because of what we only know
The rattle of those arms makes us afraid.

'We thread the needles' eyes, and all we do
All must together do.' That done, the man
Took up the nearest and began to sew.

'Now must we sing and sing the best we can,
But first you must be told our character:
Convicted cowards all, by kindred slain

'Or driven from home and left to die in fear.'
They sang, but had nor human tunes nor words,
Though all was done in common as before;

They had changed their throats and had the throats of birds.
(*CP,* 339–40)

Part II

M. L. Rosenthal

Poems of the Here and the There

The faith that the nature and methods of art will guide us more surely to the truth of man's condition than any other approach has many facets. Nothing could be more inaccurate than to conceive of this kind of aestheticism as a mere "escape," or as a trifling absorption in "lovely" effects of one kind or another. Long before he could have been fully aware of his ultimate directions, Yeats had been experimentally juggling opposites, particularly the world of the "real" and the world of imagination, the worlds of the Here and the There. He wrote on conventional subjects, yet through them was forever engaged in this balancing and blending and distinguishing. The preoccupation brought him to uneasy revelations that revived old themes and symbols and gave them new settings.

"The Stolen Child," originally published in 1886, is an interesting example, a liquidly delicate poem on the luring away of a child by faeries. The primary elements of this familiar situation of folklore are presented: the supernatural beings and the living child they entice away. But none of the familiar denouements occurs. Yeats does not tell us whether the child dies, is replaced by a changeling, or returns the "next day" an old man. Against the warm, comforting associations of landscape and of the home the child abandons, we see the faery world bathed in a sinister light. At the beginning we find the "flapping herons" and "drowsy water-rats" and hoarded "stolen cherries" of that world only

From The Modern Poets: A Critical Introduction *by M. L. Rosenthal, pp. 35–40. Copyright © 1960 by M. L. Rosenthal. Reprinted by permission of Oxford University Press, Inc.*

vaguely disturbing. In the second stanza there is something more troubled and furtive in the picture of the faeries' moonlight revels, "mingling hands and mingling glances," on the "dim grey sands." These apprehensions are brought to a climax in the third stanza as the faeries tell how they bring "unquiet dreams" ("*evil* dreams" in the poem's first version) to the slumbering trout while the ferns

> drop their tears
> Over the young streams.

The image, so reminiscent of Blake, prepares us for the pathetic seduction of the "solemn-eyed" child from his home at the end of the poem. He does not know that the faery refrain is as true for them as for him: *"the world's more full of weeping than you can understand."*

The ambiguity of this refrain suggests a new turn on an old Romantic motif: the pathos of the unattainable. Yeats adds something hinted at but never developed in Blake's "Ah! Sun-Flower" and in a few other poems. The ultimate frustration of the Romantic ideal becomes the possibility that, if we *were* allowed to pass over to the There, we should not escape the sorrows of the Here, but merely find them eternalized. Keats does not question his blissful state for the brief time that he is one with the nightingale, nor does Coleridge question the delight that would be his could he but once again recapture his vision of the "damsel with a dulcimer." But "The Stolen Child" may actually be considered a complaint against the dream of perfection itself. That dream is deceptive; it prevents realization of the attainable; it calls into question the value of everything man plans or does.

The complaint is made explicit in another early poem, "The Man Who Dreamed of Faeryland." The hero of this poem is an ordinary person who might have found measurable, if mediocre, pleasure in a commonplace love and marriage, or in money making, or in taking revenge on his enemies. Instead, each time he reaches for one of these satisfactions he is tormented by the dream of perfection. Even after his death he is so tormented that he finds "no comfort in the grave." Everywhere insignificant bits of mortality—a pile of tiny fish at a market, a clump of knot-grass, some worms—have sung to him of an existence entirely unlike the drab and paltry one they themselves represent. But of what use has the dream been to one who is in any case one of "those lovers that no lovers miss"?

In "The Lake Isle of Innisfree," the poet begins by toying whimsically with the idea of an Earthly Paradise. There *is* such an island, and he had dreamed, he elsewhere tells us, of imitating Thoreau and going to live, once he had "conquered bodily desire," on this island whose name so happily suggests freedom and inwardness. The opening rather blithely parodies Thoreau's prescription for the simple life in the woods. He will use only clay and wattles for his cabin, will plant exactly nine bean-rows, will have the music of honey bees around him—no other kind. Never mind why these preferences! But even more than in "The Stolen Child," the tone grows progressively more serious until, in the closing stanza, it conveys a really somber picture of the speaker as he stands on the "pavements grey" of the Here, haunted by an inward image of his deprivation: "I hear it in the deep heart's core." Like "The Man Who Dreamed of Faeryland," this is not only a Romantic poem but also a criticism of the Romantic dream itself.

Perhaps the most beautiful of the earlier poems on this theme is "Who Goes with Fergus?" Like the faeries summoning the child, still uninitiated into the promise of his mind and body, to "the waters and the wild" of their own eerie existence, the speaker here seems to be calling attention to the dilemma of those who would escape into the region of dreams. Ostensibly he seeks to lure the youth and the maiden into this region, over which Fergus, the great king who has forsaken his former earthly power, now reigns. Actually, he is warning them.

> Who will go drive with Fergus now,
> And pierce the deep wood's woven shade,
> And dance upon the level shore?
> Young man, lift up your russet brow,
> And lift your tender eyelids, maid,
> And brood on hopes and fear no more.
>
> And no more turn aside and brood
> Upon love's bitter mystery;
> For Fergus rules the brazen cars,
> And rules the shadows of the wood,
> And the white breast of the dim sea
> And all disheveled wandering stars.

In Fergus's realm all should be calm and joyous as in a woven hanging. It is the realm of art as well as of the dream, where youth and maid need "brood on hopes and fear no more." But the imagery of escape becomes increasingly disturbed. "White breast of the dim sea" and "disheveled wandering stars" suggest no diminution of desire or of its frustrations, but only their endless continuance.

Very early, then, Yeats begins to use the method of setting

interpenetrating opposites against one another as a deliberate way of discovering the character of the human predicament and of exploring the challenge it offers. As one reads his *Autobiography* and other writings, one is recurrently struck by his almost professionally practical attitude toward the uses of supernatural symbolism. Besides folklore, he was interested in theories of the occult from Rosicrucianism to spiritualism and mystical idealism of every sort, including that of Plato and Plotinus. His attraction to these cults and doctrines had many motivations, but one was overriding: a belief that they provided valuable clues to the unconscious life of mind and spirit and therefore to the sources of creative imagination. He sought a kind of antiscientific science whose touchstones were the "truths" of myth and art, a science that would therefore—from a poet's standpoint, at least—go beyond the materialistic thought systems prevailing in his youth and the vague bodiless religiosity that shuddered away from them. He wished, he wrote, to be able to "hold in a single thought reality and justice"—the difficult "reality" of experience and the "justice" of pure vision [*V,* 25].

"Pure vision" in Yeats is strangely related to ordinary experience. The world of symbols is not a humane or humanly ordered world, but men in their animal lives as well as in their aspirations are as it were its raw materials. As we have already seen, it is charged with the sexual principle. (The interpenetrating cones or gyres by which Yeats diagramed the great cycles of thought and personality are a sexual abstraction in themselves.) Yeats reverts again and again to the great paradox and mystery of our conscious life:

> But Love has pitched his mansion in
> The place of excrement. [*CP,* 255]

A list of his most famous poems calls up a series of vibrant, archetypal symbols revolving about the sexual mystery: the rape of Leda; a Sphinx-like beast "moving its slow thighs" over the desert as the annunciation reordering man's destiny; an old whore shrieking beautiful obscene profundities at a doctrinaire priest; an Earthly Paradise in which the great sages and heroes of tradition take their whimsical ease while the New Testament Innocents "relive their death" again and again and "nymphs and satyrs copulate in the foam" [*CP,* 211, 184, 254, 324]. In all these instances pure vision is inseparable from its physical origins:

Those masterful images because complete
Grew in pure mind, but out of what began?
A mound of refuse or the sweepings of a street,
Old kettles, old bottles, and a broken can,
Old iron, old bones, old rags, that raving slut
Who keeps the till. Now that my ladder's gone,
I must lie down where all the ladders start,
In the foul rag-and-bone shop of the heart. [*CP.* 336]

So wrote Yeats within a year of his death at seventy-four, still very much engaged with the dual principle of human consciousness, the Here and the There. At about the same time he observed that to him all things seemed "made of the conflict of two states of consciousness, beings or persons which die each other's life, live each other's death. That is true of life and death themselves" [*L,* 918]. He had been thinking in this way for many years, pushing into the heart of life by means of this interplay of opposites: "two cones (or whirls)," he called them, "the apex of each in the other's base." His early poems hint at this conflict and interplay—the youth and the maiden of *this* life, and the inhabitants of Fergus's world in *that* life, partake of one another's destinies, for example. But as Yeats grew older he used larger canvases, with bolder and more intimate detail. Thus, in the famous "Sailing to Byzantium" the speaker is an old man between two worlds. Or rather, he is deep within this world, which has all but rejected him and which he now wishes to repossess in a new way—by becoming part of a world of pure creativity in which the fleshly is transformed into the eternal. In four stanzas of eight lines each, the poet contrasts the two "countries": the sensual realm of "fish, flesh, or fowl," of "the young in one another's arms" and the raging life cycle; and the world of "unaging intellect," of the "artifice of eternity," symbolized by "the holy city of Byzantium." In *this* world stands an old man with his heart, still "sick with desire," "fastened to a dying animal." In *that* stand the "sages" beyond death in "God's holy fire," whom the speaker implores to teach his soul to sing louder than the "sensual music" by which he is here surrounded. Two worlds, two kinds of music, two sets of inhabitants, and the speaker between the two, seeking to make them one in his own person. It is man who has created the monuments of his soul's magnificence, but it is these monuments—his great works of art and thought, his spiritual creations, perhaps even God himself—which are needed now to carry him beyond the desperate moment in which he faces his own mortality.

A great deal can be "learned" from "Sailing to Byzantium" about attitudes toward death, sex, old age, and art. But whatever we thus learn is incidental to the terrible, blazing confrontation of the two spheres of being, each remote from the other yet inseparable from it. Yeats does not argue with or attempt to explain the human condition, nor does he subordinate to any specific doctrine his poem's anguished prayer for an ideal real enough to encompass and transform the speaker's experience and predicament. The poem comes close to pure symbolism, in the free play it allows thought and feeling over images of the widest possible relevance.

Balachandra Rajan

Questions of Apocalypse

Political and personal passion combine in "No Second Troy," the most celebrated poem in the collection [*The Green Helmet and Other Poems*]. It starts with an explosive question:

> Why should I blame her that she filled my days
> With misery . . . [*CP,* 101]

and the manner in which the overflow completes and alters something which had seemed already complete in the first line is typical of the kind of suspense achieved in the poem's rhetorical management. Until the last line it is uncertain which way the flood of anger will turn. The petty violence of those who would "hurl the little streets upon the great" is scornfully judged and found wanting; but it is only at the climax that the failure snaps into place. Similarly Maud Gonne is seen in terms of destruction. Her beauty is like a tightened bow, her mind made simple as a fire by nobleness. Simplicity is not a quality one associates with fire, though for Yeats the association was important enough for him to remember it much later in *Vacillation.* Here the word is potent in suggesting how uncompromising intensity and dedicated single-mindedness are capable of being both noble and, in terms of a practical world, naive. The tightened bow further suggests an inherent tension in heroic beauty that necessarily issues in destructiveness. But the implication can still be that heroic beauty cannot avoid its consequences, that it must not be blamed because it cannot help itself. Once again it is not until the twist of the last line that the images

From W. B. Yeats: A Critical Introduction *by Balachandra Rajan, pp. 68–69, 119–22, 132–34. Copyright © 1965 by Balachandra Rajan. Reprinted by permission of Hutchinson Publishing Group, Ltd.*

lock securely into their pattern. The organising thrust is cleverly withheld and the marching suspense of the monosyllables in the eleventh line, with "why," "what" and "what" reiterating the accumulated questions, is a brilliant piece of dramatic maneuvering. Then the Helen image strikes into the poem, asking the last question which the whole structure has answered, putting everything in its predestined order. It is the first demonstration, and an impressive one, of a technique which Yeats was to bring to its perfection in "The Second Coming" and "Leda and the Swan."

Admiration for "No Second Troy" need not blind us to its shortcomings. The purpose of civilisations is not to provide bonfires for eternal or heroic beauty and Ireland has not failed because it failed to be Ilium. Certainly the poem rests on a convention, but the best poems scrutinise as well as assert their conventions. It is not unfair to describe the poem as rhetoric and its vulnerability is evident from such lines as the tenth, where the rhetoric falters in propulsive power. At the same time the momentum and driving force of the poem are reminders that rhetoric has its place though not the highest of places.

* * *

"The Second Coming" is one of the half-dozen or so poems by Yeats which specifically mention gyres. His restraint in using this technical term is significant and in fact no special knowledge is needed to respond to the sense of circling, inexorable movement which the first line conveys, both through the repetition of "turning" and the fourfold repetition of the *in* sound. "Widening" suggests first the increasing scope of the movement and, in conjunction with the next line, its increasing uncontrollability. The sound echo between "falcon" and "falconer" dramatises the growing loss of contact. The next line extends disintegration from the circumference to the core. The centre cannot hold and the forces of disorder, previously only deaf to the voice of the falconer, now become eruptively dominant. "Mere anarchy is loosed upon the world"; the word "loosed" finely conveys both the ebbing power of coherence at the centre, and the unleashing of destruction as an active, rending force. "Mere anarchy," with its suggestion of worse things to come, is carried to a climax in "blood-dimmed tide," an image potent in its fusion of blind passion with apocalyptic, world-destroying violence. Against these catastrophic forces, the ceremony of innocence is a frail dyke indeed and the very word "ceremony" helps to suggest the almost formal character of the resistance. The stanza drives to a conclusion which might seem a piece of generalising, were it not for the rage of imagination behind it. Backed up by the poem, it is decisively, angrily concrete. The wisdom of the best, the centre of conviction, the moral basis of order has collapsed; the world lies open to the "passionate intensity" of those who plunge forward on the blood-dimmed tide.

The tide, with its evocations of the deluge and the flood, prepares us for an impending revelation; and the expectation is strengthened by the repetition of certain key phrases—"Surely," "is at hand," and "the Second Coming." Carefully controlled repetition is in fact an important feature of the poem, and is clearly intended to carry a certain sense of history into the poem's tactics. The Second Coming itself is repetition with a difference.

As the poem moves into the dimensions of prophecy, the shape of its revelation is established with ominous vagueness. The image out of *Spiritus Mundi* is vast not only in sheer size, but because it is beyond comprehension, because its consequences have still to be fully grasped. It troubles the sight—the word with its almost physical sense of an effort to focus, conveys not only the fitful, elusive character of revelation but the grim implications of the revelation itself. "Somewhere in sands of the desert" leaves the location purposefully vague, while the wave-like motion realises with poetic accuracy the landscape of undulating desert sand. The shape with lion body and the head of a man could, in a different context, suggest the union of power and intelligence, but the first stanza has foreclosed this possibility and the next line moves the shape forward into a frame of mindless and merciless violence. Searchers after the System may find it difficult to reconcile a "gaze blank and pitiless as the sun" with an antithetical-lunar dispensation, but the image remains threateningly appropriate to those who believe that the poem has its own rights. "Moving its slow thighs" once again conveys with Yeats' unfailing immediacy, the clumsy, powerful, stirring of the shape into life. The shadows of the desert birds reel away from it in the giddiness of nightmare but also because, accustomed as they are to death, they find themselves in a presence from which they are obliged to recoil. As the darkness drops over the desert of prophecy, we realise that every civilisation chooses its executioner. Every order, because it is order, has its own shape of exclusion, but the things it excludes must one day rise to destroy it. Each stony sleep creates its specific nightmare and, in the rocking cradle, looks on the birth of its death. The shape moves into ferocious actuality, each monosyllable a step forward by the rough beast, with the *ou* sound four times repeated, conveying with almost tactile immediacy the shambling progress of the nightmare into life. Even the word "Bethlehem" with its evocations of love and mercy is almost spat out in the run of the verse. The grim authenticity of the last lines is profound evidence of the poem's loyalty to its logic, of its determination not to stop short of total honesty.

The impact of "The Second Coming" derives from its archetypal power, a power that takes the poem beyond its "thought," into a deeper world of mythical embodiment. Even the genesis of the poem reveals its thrust towards the archetypal; Stallworthy's presentation [in *Between the Lines*] of the various manuscript drafts shows how specific references to Pitt, Burke and the German advance into Russia were discarded and how, in its evolution, the poem moved steadily to its twin objectives of universality and immediacy. Yeats himself seems to have been prepared to learn something from the poem. His original note saw in it the end of "our scientific, democratic, fact-accumulating, heterogeneous civilisation" [*VP,* 823–25] and there is nothing to suggest that he regretted the ending. Later, however, the poem became symbolic to him of "the growing murderousness of the world" and in 1938 he was quoting it to Ethel Mannin as evidence of his attitude to fascism: "Every nerve trembles with horror at what is happening in Europe."[1] *A Vision* [,] which describes an antithetical dispensation as "expressive, hierarchical, multiple, masculine, harsh, surgical" [,] seems to inherit something from the rough beast and Yeats' comment that "a civilisation is a struggle to keep self-control" is acted out in the first stanza of the poem with an authenticity unattainable even in poetic prose. The poem lives outside the philosophic texts and, if anything, illuminates those texts; but it is always considerable more than the texts. At the critical moment, Yeats tells us, "the *Thirteenth Cone,* the sphere, the unique intervenes" [*V,* 263]. It has to be so with the poetic imagination at its most creative.

* * *

"Leda and the Swan," one of the most unimprovable poems ever written, is the final fusion of history, myth and vision. Using the sonnet form, which is employed traditionally for love and public issues, Yeats writes a poem which is about both and neither. Except for the daringly judged break in the eleventh line, the formal requirements are rigorously observed and the great power of compression, which can force such massive themes into so

[1] *A,* 130; *L,* 851. (The letter to Ethel Mannin was written in 1936, not 1938.)

brief and tightly controlled a compass, finds its reward in the power and richness of the poem. Yeats did not come to this perfection easily. Ellmann shows that at least six stages of revision were needed and that it was not until the second published version that Yeats achieved the onslaught of the first line, the "sudden blow," the impact of which is the poem.

Melchiori tells us that the sources of Yeats' sonnet include, besides Michelangelo, "*the Hypnerotomachia,* Spenser, Shelley, Pater, Moreau, Blake and the Theosophists." Other scholars have suggested alternatives and the search for pictorial origins, in particular, has been pursued with a zeal that makes one wonder whether the anatomy of Leda is truly to be found in the art galleries of Europe. It is not simply that everything that enters the poem is transformed in its creativeness so that, like all great art, it is radically unlike the elements it absorbs. The poem also lives in its immediacy so that whatever it means must be reached through its impact. Bird and woman blot out the Babylonian mathematical starlight and Yeats himself tells us that as he wrote "Leda" all politics went out of it.[2]

From the very beginning the line of attack is plain. The "sudden blow" (replacing the indecisive "hoverings" of earlier drafts), the "dark webs" with their suggestion of an irresistible, inscrutable fate (superseding the needless anatomical detail of "webbed toes"), the "great wings" contrasted in their power with the "staggering," "helpless" girl and the enfolding movement of the fourth line (reinforced by the repetition of "breast"), all suggest a controlled and crushing violence, indifferent to everything but its apocalyptic function. Then the second stanza moves us into Leda's stunned acquiescence with "vague," "feathered," "loosening" and "white rush" progressively suggesting her collapse of identity while driving onward the basic assault of the poem. The inescapable contrast is between power and helplessness; and the recognition made violently real by the poem is that any revolutionary change in the direction of history must seem *at the point of change,* to be the product of superior and, indeed, overwhelming force. The virgin is always fierce and empires must always stand appalled whenever she calls out of the fabulous, formless darkness [see *CP,* 210]. The "strange heart" which takes over Leda's being does so in the moment of death which is the quick of all crisis.

The turn into the sestet is masterfully contrived with the

[2] *VP,* 828. The references in these two paragraphs are to Ellmann's *Identity of Yeats,* pp. 176–79, and Melchiori's *The Whole Mystery of Art,* pp. 73–132. (See Bibliography.)

sound shuddering through the ninth line, out of the act and into its consequences. The movement into time reveals starkly that violence is the fruit of violence while the obvious overtones of "broken wall" and "burning roof" link the future firmly to the foreground. The break in the eleventh line is not so much a return to the present as a movement from embodiment to questioning; the question is asked because the poem has both created and answered it.

> Being so caught up,
> So mastered by the brute blood of the air,
> Did she put on his knowledge with his power
> Before the indifferent beak could let her drop? [*CP,* 212]

The repeated *so* ought not to be evaded. It is not in the abstract, but in the context of the poem's actual onslaught, that the reader's judgement is required to be made; and the forces that have "caught up" and "mastered" Leda have never been presented as other than irresistible, apocalyptic violence. The double savagery of "brute blood," underlined by the alliteration and the two meanings of blood, is typical in directing our response; and the slack, detumescent monosyllables of the last line are indicative both of lust satisfied and a historical purpose fulfilled. Time and thought may make the proportions different but in the crisis, in the explosion of truth, every annunciation is revealed in power and terror.

C. K. Stead

Politics as Drama

"Easter 1916," written to commemorate the 1916 rising against the British occupation of Ireland, is one of the finest of Yeats's public poems. It is a complex poem which, more than illustrating Yeats's achievement of objectivity by means of the dramatic "mask," uses the terms of drama in order to stylize and objectify the world of political fact which is its subject. In the writing of this poem literary problems have become, for Yeats, analogues for the problems of living: "Life" and "Art" interact and merge into a single image.

The first three sections of the poem look backward to a "comic" world that has been left behind—a world of restless individuality, of mutability, subject to death and re generation. The fourth section points forward to a world of tragic stasis, achieved by those killed in the rising. Thus the movement of the poem—from the temporal to the timeless—and the intermediate position of Yeats's persona in that movement, make the poem a forerunner of the more famous "Sailing to Byzantium."

The opening lines of the poem present the "comic" Dublin scene before the Easter rising:

> I have met them at close of day
> Coming with vivid faces
> From counter or desk among grey
> Eighteenth century houses.
> I have passed with a nod of the head
> Or polite meaningless words,

From "W. B. Yeats, 1895–1916" in The New Poetic: Yeats to Eliot *by C. K. Stead, pp. 35–40. Copyright © 1964 by C. K. Stead. Reprinted by permission of Hutchinson Publishing Group, Ltd.*

Or have lingered awhile and said
Polite meaningless words. . . .

These, whom Yeats met "at close of day," are the Irish patriots, shaped in the world of modern commerce ("from counter or desk") which came into being with "grey eighteenth century" reason. Dublin is part of the civilization that followed when "the merchant and the clerk,/Breathed on the world with timid breath" [*CP,* 95]—a fragmented society, where "polite meaningless words" serve in place of collective spiritual enterprise. "Doubtless because fragments broke into ever smaller fragments" Yeats [wrote], "we saw one another in the light of bitter comedy" [*A,* 130]. The "vivid faces" of the patriots could never, it seemed, assume the static mask of tragedy. So the persona of this poem recalls his certainty

that they and I
But lived where motley is worn.

But we are warned:

All changed, changed utterly:
A terrible beauty is born.

Comedy, Yeats suggests in an essay, accentuates personality, individual character; tragedy eliminates it in favour of something universal: ". . . tragedy must always be a drowning and breaking of the dykes that separate man from man, and . . . it is upon these dykes comedy keeps house . . ." [*E&I,* 241].

The second section of the poem sketches the personalities of some of the nationalists before their destruction in the Easter rising. One, beautiful when young, had spoiled her beauty in the fervour of political agitation; another was a poet and schoolteacher; a third had shown sensitivity and intellectual daring; a fourth had seemed only "a drunken vainglorious lout." But the "dykes that separate man from man" have now been broken. Each has "resigned his part/ In the casual comedy . . ./ Transformed utterly;/ A terrible beauty is born."[1]

So far the change seems all achievement: the petty modern comedy has given way to tragic beauty. But this is also a "*terrible* beauty," beauty bought only at the expense of life:

[1] Cf. [the *Autobiography,* p. 132]: "I had seen Ireland in my own time turn from the bragging rhetoric and gregarious humour of O'Connell's generation and school, and offer herself to the solitary and proud Parnell as to her anti-self, buskin followed hard on sock. . . ." [Stead's note]

Hearts with one purpose alone
Through summer and winter seem
Enchanted to a stone
To trouble the living stream.
The horse that comes from the road,
The rider, the birds that range
From cloud to tumbling cloud,
Minute by minute they change;
A shadow of cloud on the stream
Changes minute by minute;
A horse hoof slides on the brim,
And a horse plashes within it;
The long-legged moor-hens dive,
And hens to moor-cocks call;
Minute by minute they live:
The stone's in the midst of all.

This third section is a general image of the world subject to time and death ("minute by minute they live")—an image which implies another, kindlier way of seeing the Dublin street before the rising. The nationalists have transcended the mutable word, but only by the destruction of normal human values, by a single-mindedness that turns the heart to stone. The movement of this section imparts the joy of life, which throws a new light on the "terrible beauty," emphasizing terror over beauty. The events are thus presented with an ambiguity which does justice to their complexity.

"Nations, races, and individual men," Yeats tell us

> are unified by an image, or bundle or related images, symbolical or evocative of the state of mind which is, of all states of mind not impossible, the most difficult to that man, race or nation; because only the greatest obstacle which can be contemplated without despair rouses the will to full intensity. [*A,* 132]

The "most difficult" image which the nationalists have contemplated "without despair" is that of a united, independent Ireland. But there is another way of looking at their aspirations:

We had fed the heart on fantasies,
The heart's grown brutal from the fare; [*CP,* 202]

Approval and disapproval, delight and disappointment, lie behind the poem. Out of the tensions in Yeats's own mind a complex image is generated. We know from what Maud Gonne has written that Yeats hated in her the passionate intensity that turned the heart to stone. "Standing by the seashore in Normandy in September 1916 he read me that poem ["Easter 1916"]; he had worked on it all the night before, and he implored me to forget the stone and its inner fire for the flashing, changing joy of life" [*Scattering Branches,* pp. 31–32].

But it was Yeats as a man who urged her to abandon her patriotic intensity. As a poet his task was more difficult: to make an image that would encompass the event, transcending mere "opinion"—his own, and that of others. To achieve this he must transcend himself, giving up his personality as the revolutionaries gave up life, in order to achieve the mask of tragedy. At this level the writing of the poem becomes an analogue for the event which is its subject. Yeats is caught up in the play, and must move with it. He can no longer take pleasure in "a mocking tale or a gibe" at the nationalists' expense, for he is no longer "where motley is worn." Nor can he pass judgement: "That is heaven's part." "Our part" is only that of chorus—

> our part
> To murmur name upon name,
> As a mother names her child
> When sleep at last has come
> On limbs that had run wild.

At whatever human expense, a new symbol of heroism has been created. For good or ill

> MacDonagh and MacBride
> And Connolly and Pearse
> Now and in time to be,
> Wherever green is worn,
> Are changed, changed utterly.

The Irish mind carries a new symbol, and Irish literature a new poem: there is a new stone resisting the flow of the stream. Such an achievement constitutes a defeat over the mutable world. The personalities of principal actors and chorus—of all those whose interaction created the play—are irrelevant to the effect. The world is, for the moment in which the event is contemplated, "transformed utterly."

Yeats stands alone among English speaking poets of this century in his ability to assimilate a complex political event into the framework of a poem without distortion of the event or loss of its human character in abstraction. It [is] . . . worth keeping "Easter 1916" in mind when we . . . consider the English poets of the First World War. Of them, the patriots are absurdly partisan, abstract and rhetorical; while the disillusioned soldier poets—though more admirable than the patriots because their poems come from honest feeling and particular experience—are too closely involved in the destruction to be capable of transforming these things, as Yeats transforms them, into a universal image. It is—in terms of the metaphor I have used in my Introduction [to *The New Poetic: Yeats to Eliot*]—a matter of establishing a correct distance between the poet and his subject. The soldier poets stand too close to their subject, the patriots at too great a distance. Yeats's dramatic "mask" is a means of holding himself at a correct distance.[2] He had pored long enough over the slow fires of his own and others' art, to know that death in itself is a commonplace; but that particular death, transformed in poetry to an object of contemplation, becomes a symbol—a way of understanding and expressing the human condition.

In "Easter 1916" Yeats has already achieved a solution—one solution—to a problem which had bedeviled poetry for many years: the problem of how a poem could enter the public world without losing itself in temporal "opinion." "Easter 1916" is not a pure Symbolist poem, for it is capable of discursive paraphrase; but no paraphrase can use up the poem's life. The event which is its subject is not described, but re-fashioned. There is no question of simply praising heroism or blaming folly. The men of the poem are all dead—"all changed, changed utterly"—no longer men at all but symbols that take life in the mind. Yeats leaves his personality, his opinions, behind. He puts on the mask of tragic chorus, and out of the slow impersonal contemplation of a particular event in which idealism, folly, heroism, and destructiveness were intermixed, fashions an image which stands for all such events in human history.[3]

[2] Cf. Yeats writing of two of his contemporary poets in *The Boston Pilot,* 23 April 1892. "The din and glitter one feels were far too near the writer [John Davidson]. He has not been able to cast them back into imaginative dimness and distance. Of Mr Symons' method . . . I have but seen stray poems and judge from them that, despite most manifest triumphs from time to time, he will sometimes fail through gaining too easily that very dimness and distance I have spoken of. He will, perhaps, prove to be too far from, as Mr Davidson is too near to, his subject." *Letters to The New Island,* p. 147. [Stead's note]

[3] For a recent discussion of "Easter 1916" as both a projection of the poet's inner debate and a great "public" poem, see Thomas R. Edwards, *Imagination and Power: A Study of Poetry on Public Themes,* Oxford University Press, New York, 1971, pp. 185–97.

Thomas R. Whitaker

Dramatic Experience and Panoramic Vision: "Nineteen Hundred and Nineteen"

[A central] poem about the darkening flood of history, "Nineteen Hundred and Nineteen" . . . combine[s] the perspectives of dramatic experience and panoramic vision. . . . The utterance arises from the pressure of history in modern Ireland, . . . the speaker see[ing] his dramatic moment as part of a long historical process. . . . As in some apocalyptic visions of the nineties, the speaker contemplates the end of an era, tries to come to terms with the destructive forces of history, and even longs for annihilation. . . .

Because the title of "Nineteen Hundred and Nineteen" reminds us of the Black-and-Tan terrorizing the Irish countryside, we know at the outset that the panoramic perspective of the first stanza cannot be objective but must be shaped by the speaker's awareness of his own situation:

> Many ingenious lovely things are gone
> That seemed sheer miracle to the multitude,
> Protected from the circle of the moon
> That pitches common things about. There stood
> Amid the ornamental bronze and stone
> An ancient image made of olive wood—
> And gone are Phidias' famous ivories
> And all the golden grasshoppers and bees.

He points to Phidian Athens with a familiarity of tone born of his own sense of intimacy and even "possession"—but also with a

From "Resurrected Gods" in Swan and Shadow: Yeats's Dialogue with History *by Thomas R. Whitaker, pp. 222–232.* *Copyright © 1964 by The University of North Carolina. Reprinted by permission.*

strange note of deprecation that is not simply aristocratic nonchalance. We see the ideal harmony of Doric and Ionic or European and Asiatic: the strength and solidity of "bronze and stone" and the brilliance and intricacy of ivory and gold. But the Asiatic qualities of "ingenious lovely things" are dominant. Bronze and stone are "ornamental"; "ivories" hardly suggests the monumental quality of the chryselephantine Zeus or Athene; and the "golden grasshoppers and bees," yet more delicate, provide the climax. The golden honeycomb of Daedalus, according to Pater, symbolizes the Asiatic element in the Greek synthesis; the golden grasshoppers, according to Thucydides, are symptomatic of the Athenians' degeneration from Spartan to Ionic qualities, as they laid aside their arms and adopted the luxurious ways of peace.[1] In this speaker's retrospective view, then, Athenian art seems to indicate a self-deceptive and effete ornamental culture. In the second stanza the basis for that departure from the vision of "Dove or Swan" emerges, as a bitter irony erupts:

> We too had many pretty toys when young:
> A law indifferent to blame or praise,
> To bribe or threat; habits that made old wrong
> Melt down, as it were wax in the sun's rays;
> Public opinion ripening for so long
> We thought it would outlive all future days.
> O what fine thought we had because we thought
> That the worst rogues and rascals had died out.

Something like Thucydides' critique is being sharply directed at modern British culture:

> All teeth were drawn, all ancient tricks unlearned,
> And a great army but a showy thing;

—but no genuinely peaceable society had emerged:

> What matter that no cannon had been turned
> Into a ploughshare? Parliament and king
> Thought that unless a little powder burned
> The trumpeters might burst with trumpeting

[1] Walter Pater, *Greek Studies,* London, 1910, p. 193; Thucydides, *History of the Peloponnesian War,* I.vi. The notes and source-citations in this essay have been adapted from Whitaker. Parenthetical incorporation and other devices enabled me to reduce them by half without significant sacrifice. Here and there I have cited more accessible sources and added information that may be helpful.

And yet it lack all glory; and perchance
The guardsmen's drowsy chargers would not prance.

The taste for military display suggests that violence had merely gone underground, had hidden in the deeper recesses of the self. But now the fragile and the frivolous have been swept away, and with them the facile and self-deceptive dreams of wisdom and beauty. The drawn teeth have been sown again; the seemingly drowsy psychic forces lurking below the consciousness have erupted:

Now days are dragon-ridden, the nightmare
Rides upon sleep: a drunken soldiery
Can leave the mother, murdered at her door,
To crawl in her own blood, and go scot-free;
The night can sweat with terror as before
We pieced our thoughts into philosophy,
And planned to bring the world under a rule,
Who are but weasels fighting in a hole.

With that last line, the uglier subliminal forces have been admitted even within the speaker and his fellows. The sinister shadow—"that dark portion of the mind which is like the other side of the moon" and which has prepared for "anarchic violence"[2]—has become dominant: "the nightmare/Rides upon sleep." The speaker is aware through direct experience of the destructive riding or treading of that *mara* (whether horse, fate, Lamia, or terrible mother) which, as vehicle of the erupting adverse unconscious forces, may assume social as well as individual form.

The speaker of "The Gyres" will be able to cry, "What matter though numb nightmare ride on top . . . ?" This earlier speaker, though finding no such clear "tragic joy," takes at least a step toward that exultation known when all falls in ruin:

He who can read the signs nor sink unmanned
Into the half-deceit of some intoxicant
From shallow wits; who knows no work can stand,
Whether health, wealth or peace of mind were spent
On master-work of intellect or hand,
No honour leave its mighty monument,
Has but one comfort left: all triumph would
But break upon his ghostly solitude.

[2] Yeats, *Plays and Controversies,* London, 1923, pp. v–vi.

Here, as later in "Meditations in Time of Civil War" and "Coole Park and Ballylee, 1931," the word "break" has a strange richness, suggesting both temporal loss and a partial transcendence of that loss. But how firm is that "ghostly solitude?" Is it a citadel upon which the waves of triumph would beat ineffectually, upon which the sword of triumph would be shattered—or a more fragile sanctuary which would be easily disturbed by triumph? Instead of answering such questions, the speaker immediately doubts the adequacy of his enigmatic comfort and retreats to despair:

> But is there any comfort to be found?
> Man is in love and loves what vanishes,
> What more is there to say?

But even that attempt at laconic acceptance does not quite succeed: there *is* more to say. The voice of a bitter disillusionment must add, pointing to an Athens that now carries the significance of modern Ireland as well:

> That country round
> None dared admit, if such a thought were his,
> Incendiary or bigot could be found
> To burn that stump on the Acropolis,
> Or break in bits the famous ivories
> Or traffic in the grasshoppers or bees.

The worst having been faced if not accepted, the speaker turns in Part II to a richer image than "the circle of the moon" to render the movement of history. For a moment he rises above the dramatic situation into the realm of panoramic vision alone:

> When Loie Fuller's Chinese dancers enwound
> A shining web, a floating ribbon of cloth,
> It seemed that a dragon of air
> Had fallen among the dancers, had whirled them round
> Or hurried them off on its own furious path;
> So the Platonic Year
> Whirls out new right and wrong,
> Whirls in the old instead;
> All men are dancers and their tread
> Goes to the barbarous clangour of a gong.

When historical flux is seen as artistic form, then, as in "Dove or Swan," change may be accepted and fate may be creatively danced. But though this speaker entertains such a possibility, for him the sense of coercion by the whirling dragon is still dominant. And in the last line his vision of the human dance lapses easily into an image of gong-tormented life.

The "dragon of air" becomes, in Part III, the wind of night and of winter. But after the brief contemplation *sub specie aeternitatis,* the speaker has a quiet detachment. Comfort is again in sight; he offers, in effect, a definition of "ghostly solitude."

> Some moralist or mythological poet
> Compares the solitary soul to a swan;
> I am satisfied with that,
> Satisfied if a troubled mirror show it,
> Before that brief gleam of its life be gone,
> An image of its state;
> The wings half spread for flight,
> The breast thrust out in pride
> Whether to play, or to ride
> Those winds that clamour of approaching night.

In a world of stormy flux the dialogue with the "troubled mirror" of history may at least bring self-knowledge, an image of the soul's "state." Turning on the ambiguity of that word, the stanza evokes now a condition of nobility, the easy yet defiant stateliness of the swan's "play" and its rising to meet and "ride" the opposing winds. No longer "ridden" by dragon or nightmare, the soul uses adversity to further its own flight. As hinted earlier ("He who can read the signs nor sink unmanned . . ."), adversity may bring greater vitality than do the "ingenious lovely things" of a supposedly ideal era. The speaker is now holding down *hysterica passio* at sword's point. Triumph would but "break" upon his solitude both because it is relatively weaker and because it would calm the winds which aid the soul's flight. But, as "To a Friend Whose Work Has Come to Nothing" warns, this "harder thing/Than Triumph" is "of all things known/ . . . most difficult." Because of that difficulty, in the next two stanzas the "ghostly solitude" is progressively redefined and finally overwhelmed.

> A man in his own secret meditation
> Is lost amid the labyrinth that he has made
> In art or politics;
> Some Platonist affirms that in the station
> Where we should cast off body and trade
> The ancient habit sticks,
> And that if our works could

But vanish with our breath
That were a lucky death,
For triumph can but mar our solitude.

The solitary soul is not solitary enough. Like Milton's fallen angels, it is "in wandering mazes lost," its hell the Blakean Satanic labyrinth of this life. Even death may not dissipate those self-created complexities to which it mistakenly clings, those ironically triumphant triumphs which now "can but mar" (no longer "break upon") its solitude. The sense of present self-sufficiency is waning. In a similar situation an earlier Yeatsian speaker could imagine a dreamy leap from the Satanic "nets" into a "grey twilight" where "God stands winding His lonely horn" [*CP,* 56–57]. But here:

The swan has leaped into the desolate heaven:
That image can bring wildness, bring a rage
To end all things, to end
What my laborious life imagined, even
The half-imagined, the half-written page. . . .

The swan is riding the winds of the storm, but its heaven is desolate. This is not detachment or even solitary triumph but that converse of clinging which masks the continuing impulse to cling: a destructive rage born of frustration.

Hence, though the image suggests that terrible yet ecstatic hour in "The Phases of the Moon" when "all is fed with light and heaven is bare," or that moment when Forgael can cry, "I plunge in the abyss" [*CPl,* 99], the mood remains close to that of the owl in "Meditations in Time of Civil War," who will cry her "desolation to the desolate sky." The speaker exhibits what . . . has [been] seen in Achilles, a Dionysian "passion for destruction growing out of a hatred for the destructibility of all things."[3] Instead of an acceptance of suffering and an attendant joyous freedom, the speaker knows a desire for annihilation, for the Buddhistic negation of the will which Nietzsche considered the most dangerous temptation for the Dionysian man.[4] Hence this very stanza relapses into the self-mockery that has colored the entire poem:

O but we dreamed to mend
Whatever mischief seemed
To afflict mankind, but now

[3] Rachel Bespaloff, *On the Iliad,* trans. Mary McCarthy, New York, 1947, p. 105.

[4] See *The Birth of Tragedy,* section 7; Nietzsche here reveals his own temptation by, and emancipation from, his early mentor Schopenhauer.

That winds of winter blow
Learn that we were crack-pated when we dreamed.

The attempt at transcendence a failure, the poem subsides in Parts IV and V into the exhaustion of that mood. The speaker develops the implications of the earlier perception—from which he had turned away in desiring to contemplate a nobler image of his "state"—that he and his fellows are like "weasels fighting in a hole": they themselves "Shriek with pleasure" if they show the "weasel's twist, the weasel's tooth." Like Petrie, who had mocked the learned "child who could not understand the winter" of the historical cycle,[5] he mocks the great, the wise ("They never saw how seasons run"), and the good; but he concludes by reducing himself to a status lower than that of the incendiary and bigot who "traffic in the grasshoppers or bees":

Mock mockers after that
That would not lift a hand maybe
To help good, wise, or great
To bar that foul storm out, for we
Traffic in mockery.

The "troubled mirror" of the historical moment is now showing the soul a mocking, raging, destroying image that cannot be denied. The dancers of history seem no longer mere victims of dragon or barbarous gong but accomplices. Despite its slighter drama, "Nineteen Hundred and Nineteen" contains an ethical and psychological dialectic very like that of "Meditations in Time of Civil War": a thrust the counterthrust of assertion and painful recognition that leads toward an understanding of the soul's true state. That is why, personal emotions exhausted, self-complicity in the cultural failure acknowledged, the speaker has the impersonal vision of Part VI. Again "a nature, that never ceases to judge itself, exhausts personal emotion in action or desire so completely that something impersonal . . . starts into its place, something which is as unforeseen, as completely organised, even as unique, as the images that pass before the mind between sleeping and waking. . . ."

[5] W. M. Flinders Petrie, *The Revolutions of Civilization,* London, 1911, pp. 4–5. Petrie was one of the systematic philosophers of history admired by Yeats and used by him in the construction of *A Vision.* Revealing the apparent influence upon Yeats of such men as Petrie, Henry Adams, Josef Strzygowski, Nietzsche, Pater, Spengler, and others, has been one of Whitaker's major contributions.

Dragons, nightmare, soldiery, and dancers are caught up in a visionary coda:

> Violence upon the roads: violence of horses;
> Some few have handsome riders, are garlanded
> On delicate sensitive ear or tossing mane,
> But wearied running round and round in their courses
> All break and vanish, and evil gathers head:
> Herodias' daughters have returned again,
> A sudden blast of dusty wind and after
> Thunder of feet, tumult of images,
> Their purpose in the labyrinth of the wind;
> And should some crazy hand dare touch a daughter
> All turn with amorous cries, or angry cries,
> According to the wind, for all are blind.

Though these images recall Symons' "The Dance of the Daughters of Herodias," both literary reference and meaning are richer than that echo implies. Symons' poem itself relies upon a Yeatsian, and European, convention:

> Is it the petals falling from the rose?
> For in the silence I can hear a sound
> Nearer than mine own heart-beat, such a word
> As roses murmur, blown by a great wind.
> I see a pale and windy multitude
> Beaten about the air. . . .

That apocalyptic multitude had already been envisioned in Yeats's "The Hosting of the Sidhe":

> *The winds awaken, the leaves whirl round,*
> *Our cheeks are pale, our hair is unbound. . . .*

Like Symons' daughters of Herodias, the Sidhe embody the fatal lure of immortal passion and beauty, present also in the "great wind" of Yeats's "The Secret Rose." Yeats had long known of their millennial connotations: "Sidhe is also Gaelic for wind . . . ," he said in 1899. "They journey in whirling winds, the winds that were called the dance of the daughters of Herodias in the Middle Ages, Herodias doubtless taking the place of some old goddess." Yeats was often deliberately vague in his prose notes, and he probably knew then what he did not write until 1934: that Wilde's *Salome* partly derives from Heine's depiction of Herodias in *Atta Troll,* which in turn may derive from "some Jewish religious legend for it is part of the old ritual of the year." Directly or indirectly, he might have met this Aradia, Habundia, or Diana as described by Jacob Grimm or Charles Leland.[6] In any case she entered his own myth of the triform goddess who is mother, mistress, and murderess of the solar hero. Now Herodias' daughters return as the frenzy of destructive passion, the collective nightmare, that ever brings the fall of a civilization. Loie Fuller's dancers (who had presented a Salome dance)[7] become the Sidhe; the dragon of air becomes a dusty wind.

Such images are also prophetic. "When I think of the moment before revelation," Yeats would write in "Dove or Swan," "I think of Salome . . ." [*V,* 273]. And Pater had written of Leonardo's women, in whom Yeats found the lunar beauty of the Sidhe:

> Daughters of Herodias, . . . they are not of the Christian family. . . . They are the clairvoyants, through whom, as through delicate instruments, one becomes aware of the subtler forces of nature, and the modes of their action, all that is magnetic in it. . . . Nervous, electric, faint always with some inexplicable faintness, these people seem to be subject to exceptional conditions, to feel powers at work in the common air unfelt by others, to become . . . the receptacle of them, and pass them on to us in a chain of secret influences.[8]

Here the daughters lead to a macabre revelation:

> But now wind drops, dust settles; thereupon
> There lurches past, his great eyes without thought
> Under the shadow of stupid straw-pale locks,
> That insolent fiend Robert Artisson
> To whom the love-lorn Lady Kyteler brought
> Bronzed peacock feathers, red combs of her cocks.

The blind life-denying passion of the daughters in this poem finds full expression in the repulsive vacuity of Robert Artisson. It is proper for the revelation to include "something which is as un-

[6] The prose notes quoted here (notes on "The Hosting of the Sidhe" and *The King of the Great Clock Tower*) are reprinted in *VP,* 800ff., 840. The final references are to Jacob Grimm, *Deutsche Mythologie,* and Charles Leland, *Aradia, or the Gospel of Witches.*

[7] Whitaker's note refers us to "a report of the dance in a magazine which Yeats read and to which he contributed" *(The Mask).* He mentions also "Yeats's memory of 'some Herodiade of our theatre, dancing seemingly alone in her narrow moving luminous circle'" [*A,* 215]. For further discussion of the Yeatsian "dancer," see the essays by Kermode and Donoghue, below.

[8] Pater, *The Renaissance,* London, 1910, pp. 115–16.

foreseen, as completely organised, even as unique" as this fourteenth-century minor devil and his slave of passion. But our initial shock of surprise gives way to a shock of recognition. Aside from his oblique Yeatsian ancestry (the boar without bristles in his malevolent aspect; the "shape" of the Second Coming, with "gaze blank and pitiless as the sun, . . . moving its slow thighs"), Artisson was ready to take his place in this poem. Yeats himself had earlier suggested that he might be one of the Sidhe; and Dame Alice Kyteler was virtually a human daughter of Herodias, for she was one of those witches who, according to popular belief, were called together at night by "a spirit named Herodias."[9] Her traffic with Artisson renders the human complicity in the barbaric dance of time, the abandonment of independence and dignity as man approaches the nadir of the historical cycle. Even the items of her sacrifice (according to Holinshed, "nine red cocks and nine peacocks eies")[10] were as though destined to take their place in the poem. The scream of a peacock or the crowing of a cock has often, in Yeats's work, heralded a new cycle or the entrance into eternity. But the speaker of this poem does not hear a living bird's annunciation. He sees the dismembered dead: mute testimony of time's outrage.

In "Dove or Swan" Yeats would define a civilization as "a struggle to keep self-control." It is "like some great tragic person, some Niobe who must display an almost superhuman will or the cry will not touch our sympathy. The loss of control over thought comes towards the end; first a sinking in upon the moral being, then the last surrender, the irrational cry, revelation—the scream of Juno's peacock" [*V,* 268]. The narrator of "Rosa Alchemica" similarly envisioned the end of his civilization and reflected that vision in his own soul. But because his will was weak, and because the dark forces of the abyss were correspondingly weak though decoratively elaborated, his cry barely touched our sympathy. After many more turns of Yeats's winding stair—after much controlled assimilation of those forces from beyond the ego—the speaker of "Nineteen Hundred and Nineteen" can have a stronger will and clearer perception of himself. Hence his own ethical dialectic, and no external Michael Robartes, can lead him on toward vision. Though far from "superhuman," he can gaze upon the complex image which the "troubled mirror" shows him and not sink unmanned into the half-deceit of any consolation.

[9] According to Richard de Ledrede *(A Contemporary Narrative).*
[10] Raphael Holinshed, *Chronicle of Ireland,* London, 1587, p. 69.

Part III

Frank Kermode

Dancer and Tree

I come now, having commented on some of Yeats's other dancers, to the poem in which the Dancer makes her most remarkable appearance. "Among Schoolchildren" is the work of a mind which is itself a system of symbolic correspondences, self-exciting, difficult because the particularities are not shared by the reader—but his interests are not properly in the mind but in the product, which is the sort of poetry that instantly registers itself as of the best. What I have to say of the poem should not be read as an attempt to provide another explication of it, or to provide a psychological contribution to the understanding of the poet. I have. . .a rather narrow interest in its images, and that is what I propose to pursue.

The "sixty-year-old smiling public man" of the poem is caught in the act of approving, because he has ventured out of his *genre,* of a way of educating children which. . .is completely inimical to his profoundest convictions. The tone is of self-mockery, gentle and indeed somewhat mincing, with a hint of unambitious irony—"in the best modern way," we can pick up this note without prior information, but it is at any rate interesting to know that the children are engaged in the wrong labour, the antithesis of the heroic labour of the looking-glass. The old man, because he is old and a *public* man, does not protest, but sees himself as amusingly humiliated, not too seriously betrayed, putting up with the shapelessness and commonness that life has visited upon him. But children of the kind he sees before him remind him of the great image of a lady who was all they could not hope to be, a daughter of imagination, not of memory; a daughter of the swan, the perfect em-

From Romantic Image *by Frank Kermode, pp. 82–91, 92, 96–103. Copyright © 1957 by Routledge & Kegan Paul, Ltd. Reprinted by permission of Routledge & Kegan Paul, Ltd., and Chilmark Press, Inc. (U.S. publishers).*

blem of the soul, and like Leda the sign of an annunciation of paganism and heroic poetry, for which the soul is well-lost. But she too is old; he thinks of her present image: "Did Quattrocento finger fashion it?" For even in old age she has that quality of the speaking body, the intransigent vision, perhaps, of Mantegna. And he himself had had beauty though he had spent it in his isolation and intellectual effort, and become shapeless and common, the old scarecrow of the later poems. The fifth stanza develops this theme, the destruction of the body by Adam's curse, which for Yeats is the curse of labour. It is a reworking of some lines from *At The Hawk's Well,* of ten years earlier.

> A mother that saw her son
> Doubled over with speckled shin,
> Cross-grained with ninety years,
> Would cry, 'How little worth
> Were all my hopes and fears
> And the hard pain of his birth!' [*CPl.* 137]

This old man has lain in wait for fifty years, but he "is one whom the dancers cheat"; "wisdom," conclude the singers, "must lead a bitter life," and he who pursues it prizes the dry stones of a well and the leafless tree above a comfortable door and an old hearth, children and the indolent meadows. This is the plight of the old man in the schoolroom, to be with the scarecrow thinkers and teachers and poets, out of life; the scarecrow is the emblem of such a man, because he is an absurd, rigid diagram of living flesh that would break the heart of the woman who suffered the pang of his birth.

But there are other heartbreakers, though these do not change with time, but "keep a marble or a bronze repose." "Marble and bronze" is a recurrent minor motive in Yeats. It occurs in simple form in "The Living Beauty" (1919), where there is an antithetical relationship between it and that which is truly "alive"—alive in the normal sense, and possessing that speaking body which includes the soul.

> I bade, because the wick and oil are spent,
> And frozen are the channels of the blood,
> My discontented heart to draw content
> From beauty that is cast out of a mould
> In bronze, or that in dazzling marble appears,
> Appears, but when we have gone is gone again,
> Being more indifferent to our solitude
> Than 'twere an apparition. O heart, we are old;

The living beauty is for younger men:
We cannot pay its tribute of wild tears.

These masterly verses have the seeds of much later poetry. The purpose of art, in the life of the poet, is to mitigate isolation by providing the Image which is the daily victory. "I suffered continual remorse, and only became content when my abstractions had composed themselves into picture and dramatisation. . . ." But the relief is impermanent; the poet discovers that "he has made, after the manner of his kind, Mere images" [*CP,* 160]. There is a tormenting contrast between the images (signified by the bronze and marble statuettes) and the living beauty. And out of this contrast grows the need for a poetic image which will resemble the living beauty rather than the marble or bronze. No static image will now serve; there must be movement, the different sort of life that a dancer has by comparison with the most perfect object of art. Here we see, in strictly poetic terms, a change comparable to that wrought by Pound in the abandonment of Imagism, and the development of a dynamic image-theory. The Image is to be all movement, yet with a kind of stillness. She lacks separable intellectual content, her meanings, as the intellect receives them, must constantly be changing. She has the impassive, characterless face of Salome, so that there is nothing but the dance, and she and the dance are inconceivable apart, indivisible as body and soul, meaning and form, ought to be. The Dancer, in fact is, in Yeats's favourite expression, "self-begotten," independent of labour; as such she differs totally from the artist who seeks her. She can exist only in the predestined dancing-place, where, free from Adam's curse, beauty is born of itself, without the labour of childbirth or the labour of art; where art means wholly what it *is.* The tree also means what it is, and its beauty is a function of its whole being, achieved without cost, causing no ugliness in an artist. This is one of the senses of the magnificent concluding stanza:

Labour is blossoming or dancing where
The body is not bruised to pleasure soul,
Nor beauty born out of its own despair,
Nor blear-eyed wisdom out of midnight oil.
O chestnut tree, great-rooted blossomer,
Are you the leaf, the blossom or the bole?
O body swayed to music, O brightening glance,
How can we know the dancer from the dance?

"A savoir que la danseuse *n'est pas une femme qui danse,* pour ces motifs juxtaposés qu'elle *n'est pas une femme,* mais une métaphore résumant un des aspects élémentaires de notre forme, glaive, coupe, fleur, etc., et *qu'elle ne danse pas,* suggérant, par le prodige de raccourcis ou d'eláns, avec une écriture corporelle ce qu'il faudrait des paragraphes en prose dialoguée autant que déscriptive, pour exprimer, dans la rédaction: *poéme dégagé de tout appareil du scribe.*"[1] This is Mallarmé's accurate prediction of Yeats's poem.

"Among Schoolchildren" might well be treated as the central statement of the whole complex position of isolation and the Image. Later there were many fine poems that dealt with the nature of the sacrifice, and of the fugitive victory; like "Vacillation," which asks the question "What is joy?" and answers it with an image, of a sort to be achieved only by choosing the way of Homer and shunning salvation; or like the "Dialogue of Self and Soul," or the simple statements of "The Choice":

> The intellect of man is forced to choose
> Perfection of the life or of the work,
> And if it choose the second must refuse
> A heavenly mansion, raging in the dark.
>
> When all that story's finished, what's the news?
> In luck or out the toil has left its mark:
> That old perplexity an empty purse,
> Or the day's vanity, the night's remorse.

There are poems, too, which give the problem a more specifically religious turn. The paradise in which labour and beauty are one, where beauty is self-begotten and costs nothing, is the artificial paradise of a poet deeply disturbed by the cost in labour. The ambiguities of hatred and love for "marble and bronze" inform not only those poems in which Yeats praises the active aristocratic life and its courtesies, but also the Byzantium poems, which also celebrate the paradisal end of the dilemma. In this paradise life, all those delighting manifestations of growth and change in which the scarecrow has forfeited his part, give way to a new condition in which marble and bronze are the true life and inhabit a changeless world, beyond time and intellect (become, indeed, the

[1] "It should be known that the dancer *is not a woman who dances;* for these juxtaposed motives she *is not a woman,* but a metaphor, encompassing one of the elementary aspects of our form, sword, cup, flower, etc., and *that she does not dance,* suggesting, by the wonder of skips or jumps, with a bodily writing that needs paragraphs of dialogue as well as of descriptive prose to express, in the wording: *a poem freed of every device of the scribe.*"

image truly conceived, without human considerations of cost). The artist himself may be imagined, therefore, a changeless thing of beauty, purged of shapelessness and commonness induced by labour, himself a self-begotten and self-delighting marble or bronze. "It is even possible that being is only possessed completely by the dead"; we return to the ambiguous life or death of the Image. Those who generate and die, perpetually imperfect in their world of becoming, have praise only for that world; the old man has no part in it, praising only the withered tree and the dry well, hoping only for escape into the world of complete being, the world of the self-begotten. "The artifice of eternity," like "the body of this death," is a reversible term.

"Sailing to Byzantium" could scarcely be regarded as less than a profoundly considered poem; yet Yeats was willing to accept the criticism of the acute Sturge Moore that the antithesis of the birds of the dying generations and the golden bird was imperfect; and this consideration was one of the causes of the second poem, "Byzantium." "Your *Sailing to Byzantium,*" wrote Moore, "magnificent as the first three stanzas are, lets me down in the fourth, as such a goldsmith's bird is as much nature as man's body, especially if it only sings like Homer and Shakespeare of what is past or passing or to come to Lords and Ladies." Yeats sent him a copy of "Byzantium" so that he should have an idea of what was needed for the symbolic cover design of his new book (at this time he was going to call it not *The Winding Stair* but *Byzantium*) and added that Moore's criticism was the origin of the new poem—it had shown the poet that "the idea needed exposition.". . .

. . . Yeats was . . . interested in Byzantine art [because] it gave him that sense of an image totally estranged from specifically human considerations (and particularly from discursive intellect), with meaning and form identical, the vessel of the spectator's passion, which led him to develop the Dancer image. . . . Life-in-death, death-in-life, [also characterize] the perfect being of art. The absolute difference, as of different orders of reality, between the Image and what is, in the usual sense, alive, was the crucial point upon which the first Byzantium poem had, on Moore's view, failed; it was so important to the poet that he did his work again, making the distinction more absolute, seeking some more perfect image to convey the quality, out of nature and life and becoming, of the apotheosized marble and bronze. The bird must absolutely be a bird of artifice; the entire force of the poem for Yeats depended upon this—otherwise he would scarcely have bothered about Moore's characteristic, and of course intelligent, quibble. Professor N. Jeffares has shown how full are the opening lines of "Sailing to Byzantium" of peculiarly powerful suggestions of natural life, the life of generation; the salmon carries obvious suggestions of sexual vigour, and, it might be added, of that achieved physical beauty Yeats so much admired, immense power and utter singleness of purpose, in the business of generating and dying. Of course the golden bird must be the antithesis of this, as well as the heavenly counterpart of old scarecrows. It prophesies, speaks out as the foolish and passionate need not; it uses the language of courtesy in a world where all the nature-enforced discriminations of spirit and body, life and death, being and becoming, are meaningless. "Marbles of the dancing floor/ Break bitter furies of complexity." And it is this world that Byzantium symbolises. Mr. Jeffares says the bird is different in the second poem because "here it is explicitly contrasted with natural birds, to their disadvantage." In fact the same contrast is intended in the earlier poem; the new degree of explicitness is what Moore's criticism forced upon the poet. The focus of attention is no longer on the poignancy of the contrast between nature and art in these special senses; nature now becomes "mere complexities, The fury and the mire," and the strategy of the poem is, clearly, to establish the immense paradoxical vitality of the dead, more alive than the living; still, but richer in movement than the endless agitation of becoming.

And this is precisely the concept of the dead face and the dancer, the mind moving like a top, which I am calling the central icon of Yeats and of the whole tradition. Byzantium is where this is the normal condition, where all is image and there are no contrasts and no costs, inevitable concomitants of the apparition of absolute being in the sphere of becoming. We can harm the poem by too exclusive an attention to its eschatology, and it is salutary to read it simply as a marvellously contrived emblem of what Yeats took the work of art to be. There is no essential contradiction between the readings. The reconciling force is Imagination, the creator of the symbol by which men "dream and so create Translunar paradise" [*CP,* 196]. Or, to use the completely appropriate language of Blake, "This world of Imagination is the world of Eternity; it is the divine bosom into which we shall all go after the death of the Vegetated body. This World of Imagination is Infinite & Eternal, whereas the world of Generation, or Vegetation, is Finite & Temporal. The Human Imagination. . .appear'd to Me. . .throwing off the Temporal that the Eternal might be Establish'd. . . . In Eternity one Thing never Changes into another Thing. Each Identity is Eternal" [*A Vision of the Last Judgment*]. There is no better gloss on Yeats's poem, a poem impossible outside the tradition of the Romantic Image and its corollary, the doctrine of necessary isolation and suffering in the artist.

In poems later than these, Yeats continues the search for the reconciling image; and he constantly recurs to the theme of remorse, the lost perfection of the life. His "Dejection Ode," at last, is "The Circus Animals' Desertion." The poet sought a theme, without finding one:

> Maybe at last, being but a broken man,
> I must be satisfied with my heart. . . .

The "heart" is the self, speaking out stilled fury and lifeless mire; it is that which has been denied for the work. He enumerates the old themes which had served in the past to cheat the heart, and presents them all, unfairly bitter, as the consolations merely of his own imperfection and estrangement. Oisin was sent through the islands of "vain gaiety, vain battle, vain repose" to satisfy an amorous need in the poet; *The Countess Cathleen* had its origin in a private fear for a mistress, but "soon enough/This dream itself had all my thought and love." And this was the way with all his themes.

> And when the Fool and Blind Man stole the bread
> Cuchulain fought the ungovernable sea;
> Heart-mysteries there, and yet when all is said
> It was the dream itself enchanted me:
> Character isolated by a deed
> To engross the present and dominate memory.
> Players and painted stage took all my love,
> And not those things that they were emblems of.

"Players and painted stage" are here the dream, the work of imagination which relegates "real" life to a position of minor importance. Hence the final stanza; like the fresh images of Byzantium, these images begin in fury and mire, among the dying generations, and are changed in the dream of imagination. When this no longer works, the poet falls back into the "formless spawning fury" [*CP,* 323], left to live merely, when living is most difficult, life having been used up in another cause.

> Those masterful images because complete
> Grew in pure mind, but out of what began?
> A mound of refuse or the sweepings of a street,
> Old kettles, old bottles, and a broken can,
> Old iron, old bones, old rags, that raving slut

That keeps the till. Now that my ladder's gone,
I must lie down where all the ladders start,
In the foul rag-and-bone shop of the heart.

The increasingly autobiographical quality of the later poems is justified precisely by this need to examine the relation of process to product, of dying generations to bronze and marble. We are reminded of the extraordinary proportion of biographical matter in Coleridge's poem, particularly in the first version of it.[2] If we wanted to study Yeats as hero, we could dwell upon the astonishing pertinacity with which he faced, and the integrity with which he solved, a problem which can never be far from the surface of poetry in this tradition; the Image is always likely to be withdrawn, indeed almost any normal biographical situation is likely to cause its withdrawal—this is part of its cost. Coleridge was finished as a poet in his early thirties; Arnold's situation is in this respect rather similar. Yeats often faced the crisis; the *Autobiographies* show how often, and how desperately, and many poems are made out of it. When poetry is Image, life must, as Yeats said, be tragic.

The dead face which has another kind of life, distinct from that human life associated with intellectual activity; the dancer, inseparable from her dance, devoid of expression—that human activity which interferes with the Image—turning, with a movement beyond that of life, in her narrow luminous circle and costing everything; the bronze and marble that does not provide the satisfactions of the living beauty but represent a higher order of truth, of being as against becoming, which is dead only in that it cannot change: these are the images of the Image that I have considered [here]. They culminate, in Yeats, in the Dancer-image of "Among Schoolchildren"; and so does the image of the Tree. This image summarises the traditional Romantic critical analogy of art as organism, and, while it is intimately related to the doctrine of the Image, as I have described it, one must discuss it in its own context. In a sense the next [section] will take us no further, except in so far as it clinches my reading of Yeats's "Among Schoolchildren"; but its relation to the cult of the Image is so close that it has at any rate to be mentioned, and it can be regarded as an excursus, or an attempt to consolidate.

The work of art considered as having "a life of its own," supplying its own energy, and possessing no detachable meanings—

[2] Coleridge's "Dejection: An Ode" was, in its original, unpublished version, a verse epistle to the woman he loved, Sara Hutchinson.

yielding to no analysis, containing within itself all that is relevant to itself—the work of art so described invites an analogy with unconscious organic life, and resists, not only attempts to discuss it in terms of the intention of the artist or detachable "morals" or "prose contents," but attempts to behave towards it as if it were a kind of machine. The Image, indeed, belongs to no natural order of things. It is out of organic life; but it is easier and less dangerous to talk about it in terms of the organic than in terms of the mechanical. Confusion sometimes results, as in the writings of T. E. Hulme. But philosophical exactitude is not what we are looking for. The Image is "dead, yet flesh and bone"; un-vital, yet describable, almost necessarily, in terms of vitality. . . .

. . . Now the point about such images . . . is that they are body-and-soul together, meaning what they are, possessing organic vitality because they behave like the tree and the dancer. Discourse, thinking in concepts, is, in contrast, mechanical.

Even Arnold, notorious for his insistence on the mechanical aspects of architectonic—more akin, in Coleridge's terminology, to "shape" than to "form"—and his disturbance at the bad habit of poets who concentrated on the detail rather than the design, was well aware of this organic-mechanistic antithesis. He was of course steeped in Burke, and seems to have known Coleridge's distinction between "culture" and "civilization"; and in poetry he did not want to "solve the universe" but to "reconstruct" it . . . and to get, like Shakespeare, "the movement and fulness of life itself." The work must be filled with "one interpenetrating, all-animating soul." It must have a life of its own, its life and its beauty being the same thing. It must be like a tree.

I do not suggest that Yeats himself had the historical background of the tree image in mind when he used it; and in any case the direct line of descent in his case runs not from the Germans and Coleridge but from Blake, who makes a very large contribution to Yeats's aesthetic. One may see something of this, without leaving the tree-image, by a glance at Yeats's poem "The Two Trees," published in *The Rose* (1893). This poem is obviously based on a lyric in Blake's *Poetical Sketches*—

Love and harmony combine,
And around our souls entwine,
While thy branches mix with mine,
And our roots together join.

Joys upon our branches sit,
Chirping loud, and singing sweet;

Like gentle streams beneath our feet
Innocence and virtue meet.

Thou the golden fruit dost bear,
I am clad in flowers fair;
Thy sweet boughs perfume the air,
And the turtle buildeth there.

There she sits and feeds her young,
Sweet I hear her mournful song;
And thy lovely leaves among,
There is love; I hear his tongue.

There his charming nest doth lay,
There he sleeps the night away;
There he sports along the day,
And doth among our branches play.

This is a poem of innocence; of innocent sexuality, in fact. The tree has in it no positive trace of the enormous symbolism it was later to carry in Blake, best summed up perhaps in the brief antithesis "Art is the Tree of Life. . . . Science is the Tree of Death" *(The Laocoon Group)* but it is clearly the Tree of Life. Yeats was of course interested from the start in the mature symbolism of the two Trees, for the first symbolised the creative and redemptive imagination and the second all barrenly discursive and prudential knowledge; "men who sought their food among the green leaves of the Tree of Life condemned none but the unimaginative and the idle, and those who forget that even love and death and old age are an imaginative art," as Yeats explains it in *Ideas of Good and Evil.* The good tree is desire and divine energy, the bad is morality and nature, the fallen world, selfhood and abstraction. All this symbolism Yeats is trying to incorporate in what appears an insubstantial song. He used it again in an interesting prose passage called "The Tree of Life" which is closely associated with "The Guitar Player," and which makes much of Verlaine and the argument that "We artists have taken overmuch to heart that old commandment about seeking after the Kingdom of Heaven." It is a very Blakean remark; and Yeats could always see French Symbolism in Blakean terms. His poem even imitates the movement of Blake's, but he introduces a schematic contrast between the Tree of life and the Tree of knowledge or death, which derives from the more developed symbolism of his author. Here, in very early Yeats, we have a theme closely related to that of the dancer expressed in terms of the organicist tree-analogue, yet almost completely derived from Blake.

Beloved, gaze in thine own heart,
The holy tree is growing there;
From joy the holy branches start,
And all the trembling flowers they bear.
The changing colours of its fruit
Have dowered the stars with merry light;
The surety of its hidden root
Has planted quiet in the night;
The shaking of its leafy head
Has given the waves their melody.
And made my lips and music wed,
Murmuring a wizard song for thee.
There, through bewildered branches, go
Winged Loves borne on in gentle strife,
Tossing and tossing to and fro
The flaming circle of our life.
When looking on their shaken hair,
And dreaming how they dance and dart,
Thine eyes grow full of tender care;
Beloved, gaze in thine own heart.

Here, well concealed in the Blakean simplicities that are mostly direct borrowings, are the properties of the Tree of Imagination. The branches are "holy"; they start from "joy." The tree is responsible for a universal harmony, the prerequisite of traditional symbolist systems, and also for the song of poets. It is inhabited by Love, and it grows in the heart of a woman who is beautiful and does not think. If she does so she is gazing at another Tree:

Gaze no more in the bitter glass
The demons, with their subtle guile,
Lift up before us when they pass,
Or only gaze a little while;
For there a fatal image grows,
With broken boughs and blackened leaves,
And roots half hidden under snows
Driven by a storm that ever grieves.
For all things turn to barrenness
In the dim glass the demons hold,
The glass of outer weariness,
Made when God slept in times of old.
There, through the broken branches, go
The ravens of unresting thought;
Peering and flying to and fro,
To see men's souls bartered and bought.
When they are heard upon the wind,
And when they shake their wings, alas!

Thy tender eyes grow all unkind;
Gaze no more in the bitter glass. [*CP*, 47–48]

It is needless to say how close this is to the theme of woman's beauty bartered for argument, the brawling of the marketplace bringing a shrill voice and hard eyes; beauty, whether of the body or of art, is broken by an act of homage to the abstract, as Eve bowed to the tree when she had eaten the apple. This second tree, for Yeats and Blake, is the tree of the Fall. The other is the tree of Life, the vitality of the body of the Image. It has some part in the figure of the green laurel so beautifully used in "A Prayer for My Daughter"; and after many years, when Yeats came to revise this little early poem, he made changes only to achieve more violent emphases in his later manner:

There the Loves a circle go,
The flaming circle of our days,
Gyring, spiring to and fro
In those great ignorant leafy ways—

it is not the gyres that are important here, but the emphatic "ignorant"—this is the anti-intellectualist tree.

. . . Flying, crying, to and fro,
Cruel claw and hungry throat,
Or else they stand and sniff the wind,
And shake their ragged wings. . . .

The vulture image enhances the dead rottenness of the second tree; it is one of the poems Yeats improved by revision, and the reason is probably that he had never ceased to live with its images, so early taken from Blake to become part of his own mind.

For it is a fact that nearly all Yeats's later thought develops from a position—or is intruded into a pattern—already formed when he made his edition of Blake. In the field of aesthetics this first tree is the quasi-instinctive, happy, self-begotten work of imaginative art; the second is that of the reason which, as a merely reflective faculty, partakes of death (for in this loose philosophical context the words of Blake and Coleridge are often interchangeable). In many other related ways also the relation with Blake persists. There is the fundamental insistence upon the inseparability of soul and body—"the notion that a man has a body distinct from his soul must be expunged" [*The Marriage of Heaven and Hell;* slightly misquoted]—which is reflected in Yeats's theory of education as well as in his Symbolist theory of the Image; neither the beautiful woman nor the Image she emblematizes must be surrendered to the Spectre. Similar opinions are common in Symbolist aesthetics, and were influentially stated by Gourmont (see Pound's essay on this author); but Yeats, like Symons, had already been prepared for the French theories by Blake and Pater. Similarly the practical requirements of the Symbolist artist (concreteness and the scrupulous exclusion of *insignificant* detail from the organic design) were perfectly familiar to students of Blake and his disciples, all, as Yeats said, Symbolists *avant la lettre.* Blake's conviction of the paramount importance of distinctness in perception and so in the artist's outline—and of what were for the hated Locke secondary qualities, like redness in roses, hardness in diamonds—and of what he called "minute particulars"—are echoed in Yeats. The love of clear outline, the first requirement of *Dinglichkeit,* has indeed important implications for image-theory in Blakean thinkers. "All depends on Form or Outline"; Blake constantly insists upon the need for concreteness, preferring the sharp outline of the childish perception to that control of the abstract and general that comes with maturity. But this concreteness and definition is not in nature, which for Blake is fallen; it is the gift of divine imagination. The artist *makes* the eternal world; it is the product of his Imagination. The great tree itself, the organicist image, is not, in Blakean terms a vegetable tree; if it were it would be dead. Only the imagination can make it live as a symbol, and that is the true life. Pursuing this notion in less exalted terms, Blake anticipates much modern aesthetic with his argument that conception and execution are, in the artist, the same act. "I have heard many People say, 'Give me the Ideas. It is no matter what Words you put them into,' & others say, 'Give me the Design, it is no matter for the Execution.' These People know Enough of Artifice, but Nothing of Art. Ideas cannot be Given but in their minutely Appropriate Words, nor Can a Design be made without its minutely Appropriate Execution. . . . He who copies does not Execute; he only Imitates what is already Executed. Execution is only the result of Invention" ["Public Address"]. The most notable modern defence of this position is Collingwood's. But here it is soberly expressed; and for Blake, and after him Yeats, it is more usual to think of the Imagination as divine, and as conferring symbolic concreteness, by means of what we call art, on the fallen world; "Nature has no outline, but Imagination has . . . Nature has no Supernatural and dissolves: Imagination is Eternity" [*The Ghost of Abel*]. The act of conception-execution is a symbol-making act; it confers significance, makes a live thing of which the mode of existence is not temporal at all, and which is variously represented, under different aspects, by such images as those of the Dancer and the Tree.

The artist who performs this act is a man inspired and apart; but he has no rights over the Image. Blake is completely "anti-intentionalist"; witness his remark on Wordsworth's Preface. The Wordsworth who matters was the maker of symbols—the Leech Gatherer, the tree "of many one"; these place him among the great artists. . . . The other, mechanistic Wordsworth was the sane reasonable man who failed to see that natural objects deaden and was constantly abstracting from his vision, having misunderstood his own poetry. Here are two more beliefs Yeats shared: he distrusted explanations, even his own, and he distrusted Imitation, because it is always abstraction. It is not the poet's business to reproduce the appearances of the fallen world and make abstractions from it; the sons of Albion did that when they made "an Abstract, which is a negation Not only of the Substance from which it is derived . . . but also a murderer Of every Divine member" [*Jerusalem,* plate 10]. Yeats always professed his hatred of abstraction, his adherence to the Blakean doctrine of concretion, firmness of outline; and frequently, in those excellent essays on Blake, asserted the master's teaching on Imitation. He quotes with particular approval the requirement of "distinct, sharp and wiry" bounding lines, though with the qualification that Blake, in his "visionary realism," forgot how colour and shadow may assist this prime requirement, and "compel the canvas or paper to become itself a symbol of some not indefinite because unsearchable essence"—words which link Blake with the ultimate definitions of the Symbol in Yeats's own time. Above all, Yeats was in complete sympathy with Blake's plea for the formal significance of every part of a painting or poem. That is why he studied Palmer and Calvert, and why the "touchstones" of poetic symbolism provided in the essay called "The Symbolism of Poetry" [*E&I,* 153–64] are all verses which derive their power from internal reference: their quality, that is, is dependent upon the organisms to which they belong, like the dancer upon the dance, and the blossom upon the tree. That is what distinguishes this true Symbolist writing from the wrong kind of poetry, the kind that was, he hoped, being superseded: "descriptions of nature for the sake of nature, of the moral law for the sake of the moral law . . . brooding over scientific opinion," poetry in which sense and spirit, body and soul, were dissociated.

The Tree is in a sense necessary to the Dancer, since it so powerfully reinforces the idea of integrity—"root, shoot, blossom"

[*CP,* 314]—in the Image, and provides a traditional analogy in support of the Image's independent life. It is fitting that the two emblems should have been fused in "Among Schoolchildren," where the cost in life to the artist is also so wonderfully involved. The poem is the fullest expression of Yeats's mature attitude to the whole question of art in life, and it is characteristic that its elements had been in his mind for many years, conducing to what he would have called tragedy in his life, but also towards this, the greatest of his victories over "outward fate."

The Tree in Yeats is not a merely personal symbol. He learnt it in the first place from Blake, who more than any other artist formed his mind; and it is therefore profoundly associated with the tradition in which he wrote, and with the attempt to restore to art that integrity which it could possess only if it were to become once again truly Symbolist; which is to say, recover those images of truth which have nothing to do with the intellect of scientists, nothing to do with time. They exist beyond the possibility of dissociation (even in the paraphrase of critics) in a condition of perfect unity and vitality ("integrity, consonance and clarity" said Stephen Dedalus)[3] And, though few have written about it so fully and frankly as Yeats, this is the effort of all the major poets in the Romantic tradition—and the critics too.

[3] In Joyce's *A Portrait of the Artist as a Young Man.*

Richard Ellmann

Assertion Without Doctrine

I. BELIEF

Yeats's poetry abounds in challenging statements about the world. How sympathetically these are to be taken by the reader, and how firmly they are asserted by the writer, are problems that have vexed his critics. They also vexed Yeats himself. He did not describe his assertions as statements of belief, and his not doing so is the more surprising because he freely and unequivocally criticized disbelief.

The inconsistency is only superficial. To hold certain ideas as "beliefs" would give them a sort of autonomy; the mind, whose independence Yeats demanded, would become subservient to them, instead of their being necessary expressions of it. Man would be surrounded by a group of mammoth pyramidal conceptions outside his control. But the object of Yeats's verse was . . . to eliminate just such cold-blooded relationships; an external set of ideas held as beliefs was as dangerous as an external nature. He therefore argued that the word "belief" did not belong to our age.

Yet if his statements are not beliefs, what are they? To give them a name he sometimes spoke of them as ideas which he had held for so long that he could now call them his convictions; here the test was not their philosophical validity, but the length of time the mind could encompass and cherish them. In the same vein, he referred to them as ideas which he could not help drawing on whenever he wrote. The fact that they were useful in his art was

From The Identity of Yeats *by Richard Ellmann, pp. 39–61. Copyright © 1964 by Oxford University Press, Inc. Reprinted by permission of Oxford University Press and Richard Ellmann.*

also relevant, because art would not endure them if they were nonsensical. Yeats's approach to the problem is epitomized in his remarks about immortality, an idea frequently set forth in his verse. When he defends immortality, he argues pragmatically that confidence in it is necessary to human survival; without it no course of conduct except brute pleasure-seeking would hold any attraction. He is close to Nietzsche's contention that some ideas are life-furthering and some not, and that we must hold to those that are. Yeats's second argument is also pragmatic: to those who denied immortality he was likely to point out that scepticism destroyed the integrity of the mind. These arguments are alike in that they emphasize not immortality, but man, and insist upon the mixture of ideas with other human experiences.

Yeats was encouraged to take this position, which has so contemporary a sound, by his agnostic father. John Butler Yeats held that the poet must feel disengaged from doctrine, able to use it if it suited a poetic purpose, and to abjure or modify it if it did not. He said that the poet must not attach himself so strongly to his ideas that his verse becomes bothersomely credal and to that extent unpoetic. The poem may use beliefs, but must never seem to have been written merely to express them. They must be fused, along with emotional and formal patterns, into a unit with its own autonomy, where their function as beliefs is lost or unimportant. Most critics today maintain that we do not have to share the beliefs of Dante or Milton in order to appreciate their poetry; but J. B. Yeats's contention goes further, in suggesting that neither Dante nor Milton necessarily believed what he wrote, and that if either did, he embodied his belief in his poetry for artistic and not religious reasons. . . .

But Yeats differed from his father . . . in being fascinated by belief, or rather, by the believer's stance. . . . He had a great interest in any thought which had aroused the passions of masses of men or of some small group of gifted individuals. Yet he was unable to hold it with the same enduring fervour that they had. His use of Irish fairy tales is a good example. He was much impressed by the survival in the Irish countryside of a belief in fairies. In *The Celtic Twilight* (1893) he described this and other beliefs with sympathy, but took care to explain that his own beliefs were not necessarily identical with theirs. In another of the weaving images to which he customarily resorted, he attempted to describe belief as a gradual conscious formulation of experience, a personal formulation which drew its strength not from its truth but from the energy and sufficiency of the experience:

> I have . . . been at no pains to separate my own beliefs from those of the peasantry, but have rather let my men and women, dhouls and faeries, go their way unoffended or defended by any argument of mine. The things a man has heard and seen are threads of life, and if he pull them carefully from the confused distaff of memory, any who will can weave them into whatever garments of belief please them best. I too have woven my garment like another, but I shall try to keep warm in it, and shall be well content if it do not unbecome me.[1]

The word belief is already an embarrassment to him. In later life he identified it with "the sense of spiritual reality," and, characteristically for his later manner, said that it was not the result of a slow weaving process, but "comes whether to the individual or to crowds from some violent shock." But both metaphors emphasize the intimacy and immediacy of the poet's relation to an idea.

Before he was thirty Yeats framed his principle of including statements in his verse without implying that they had any validity outside the particular poem where they appeared. . . . Beliefs had to be included in some form, but, as he wrote George Russell in 1900, poetic expression should never be compromised if it got in the way of a poet's philosophy. He argued that there could be no fundamental conflict:

> I do not understand what you mean when you distinguish between the word that gives your idea & the more beautiful word. Unless of course you merely mean that beauty of detail must be subordinate to beauty of general effect, it seems to me just as if one should say "I don't mind if my sonata is musical or not so long as it conveys my idea!" Beauty is the end & law of poetry. It exists to find the beauty in all things, philosophy, nature, passion,—in what you will, & in so far as it rejects beauty, it destroys its own right to exist. If you want to give ideas for their own sake write prose. In verse they are subordinate to beauty which is their soul if they are true. Isn't this obvious?[2]

Ideas, like nature and the passions, furnish the poet with material, and his task is to weld them into poems. Ideas which are true are those which lend themselves to this treatment. Ideas which are false or insincere remain isolated abstractions and spoil the poem;

[1] *The Celtic Twilight.* For full documentation of this essay, the student must consult *The Identity of Yeats,* pp. 302–8. I have tried to incorporate the most important sources, citing more accessible texts where possible. Much of the early material Ellmann quotes remains unpublished.

[2] For Wade's transcription, slightly different, see *L,* 343.

they divert to themselves attention which should focus on the poem of which they are only a part.

Because he wished to use ideas without being submerged by them, Yeats kept throughout his life to the dramatic lyric and the drama, where the test of an idea is not its significance outside poem or play, but its relevance to the speaker's dramatic situation. The author forgets himself in the role that he assumes in the poem; this role is not pretence, but is often a simplification and intensification of something in his mind whose presence there he may hardly have recognized. A later letter to Sean O'Casey expresses Yeats's lifelong position. It was written to explain the Abbey Theatre's rejection of O'Casey's play, *The Silver Tassie,* on the grounds that it was too full of O'Casey's own views:

> Among the things that dramatic action must burn up are the author's opinions; while he is writing he has no business to know anything that is not a portion of the action. Do you suppose for one moment that Shakespeare educated Hamlet and King Lear by telling them what he thought and believed? As I see it Hamlet and Lear educated Shakespeare, and I have no doubt that in the process of that education he found out that he was an altogether different man to what he thought himself, and had altogether different beliefs. A dramatist can help his characters to educate him by thinking and studying everything that gives them the language they are groping for through his hands and eyes but the control must be theirs, and that is why the ancient philosophers thought a poet or dramatist Daimon-possessed. [*L,* 741]

To be successful the poet must be humble before his own *personae.*

In Yeats's verse, we shall find, a series of ideas recur, but they recur as expressions of his characters. These ideas attract his characters not as conceptions external to themselves to which they owe allegiance; they are better described as necessary counters to express pride of life, defiance of vulgarity, anxiety about the future, or refusal to accept despair. The only way in which poetry can be philosophical, Yeats brilliantly declared, is by portraying "the emotions of a soul dwelling in the presence of certain ideas" [*Bookman,* 6 (August 1894)]. Without ideas at all the poet is shallow, timid, and sentimental; with ideas gripped tightly as beliefs the poet is gullible, opinionative, and biased; but with ideas as perches, or habitual surroundings, or, like the elements, symbolic counters, he is made free.

II. IDEAS OVERPOWERED

Among the recurrent ideas in his verse, the most imaginatively seductive was reincarnation. The notion that the soul passes through round after round of lives was steeped in folklore and ancient religions. It had the advantage, to a man who prided himself on iconoclasm, of being un-Christian, unscientific, and unconventional. Darwinism, on the other hand, was a creed to be disbelieved or believed like religion; and even if considered as a myth rather than a solemn scientific faith, its concern with subhuman development was of little use to Yeats, whose interest was in the highest human faculty—the imagination. "Romantic poetry," Ezra Pound has shrewdly suggested, "almost requires the concept of reincarnation as part of its mechanism. No apter metaphor having been found for certain emotional colours." Yeats adopted reincarnation in his verse not really because he needed it, or because he believed it, but because he liked it.

His interest in reincarnation was aroused very early. Perhaps through his friend Russell, who was precociously versed in all the Indian literature that had been translated, he took to reading Indian poetry such as Kalidasa's, and then Theosophical books like A. P. Sinnett's *Esoteric Buddhism.* He was aided in his studies by the visit to Dublin in 1885 of a Bengali Brahmin named Mohini Chatterjee, who came as a representative of the Theosophical Society. Yeats asked if he should pray, and the Brahmin replied: No, one should say before sleeping: "I have lived many lives, I have been a slave and a prince. Many a beloved has sat upon my knees and I have sat upon the knees of many a beloved. Everything that has been shall be again."

In making a poem out of this pronouncement, Yeats at once appreciated the danger of its seeming merely didactic. He put it into a dramatic setting by calling it "Kanva on Himself," Kanva being a fictitious Indian to whom several of the early poems were originally attributed, and had Kanva speak it as a series of rhetorical questions. Even these precautions did not save it:

> Now wherefore hast thou tears innumerous?
>   Hast thou not known all sorrow and delight
> Wandering of yore in forests rumorous,
>   Beneath the flaming eyeballs of the night,
>
> And as a slave been wakeful in the halls
>   Of Rajas and Mahrajas beyond number?
> Hast thou not ruled among the gilded walls?
>   Hast thou not known a Raja's dreamless slumber?

Hast thou not sat of yore upon the knees
  Of myriads of beloveds, and on thine
Have not a myriad swayed below strange trees
  In other lives? Hast thou not quaffed old wine

By tables that were fallen into dust
  Ere yonder palm commenced his thousand years?
Is not thy body but the garnered rust
  Of ancient passions and of ancient fears?

Then wherefore fear the usury of Time,
  Or Death that cometh with the next life-key?
Nay, rise and flatter her with golden rhyme,
  For as things were so shall things ever be. [*VP,* 723–24]

Although the image of the body as the "garnered rust" of passions has some interest, it does not compensate for the clumsy "innumerous" and "rumorous" and for the stilted and exhausted diction. The poem's failure comes largely from the lack of resistance offered in it. It is too single-minded, as if Kanva were an advocate for reincarnation as a doctrine. When, many years later, Yeats rewrote it, he demonstrated the way to make reincarnation serve the poem:

MOHINI CHATTERJEE

I asked if I should pray,
But the Brahmin said,
'Pray for nothing, say
Every night in bed,
"I have been a king,
I have been a slave,
Nor is there anything,
Fool, rascal, knave,
That I have not been,
And yet upon my breast
A myriad heads have lain."'

That he might set at rest
A boy's turbulent days
Mohini Chatterjee
Spoke these, or words like these.
I add in commentary,
'Old lovers yet may have
All that time denied—
Grave is heaped on grave
That they be satisfied—
Over the blackened earth
The old troops parade,

> Birth is heaped on birth
> That such cannonade
> May thunder time away,
> Birth-hour and death-hour meet,
> Or, as great sages say,
> Men dance on deathless feet.'

In its revised form the poem could please no orthodox Hindu. The significance of reincarnation as doctrine has abated, and the poem is much more than a statement of belief. Mohini's remarks become an assertion of the paradox that women have loved even fools, rascals, slaves, and knaves, as well as kings, that the soul will encounter during its cycle every possible state and yet always experience love. The whole poem is now argued in terms of love; the cannonade of rebirth is the desperate struggle with time to enable frustrated lovers to be satisfied. The propositions are arrived at by necessity and after struggle. Mohini, too, is no longer a wise man speaking, like Kanva, oracularly; instead his advice is motivated in part by a desire to calm his young pupil, and the pupil later is able to speak for himself with western energy. A dramatic relation is established between them.

Not only has Yeats enlivened the later poem by a sense of importunacy absent from the quietism of the earlier version, but he makes no claim upon the reader's belief, or even, to use Coleridge's term, his suspension of disbelief. In his assumed role of commentator, he explicates a text by exploding passion in the philosophical lesson. The subjunctive "that" clauses ("That they be satisfied," "That such cannonade . . .") can be clauses of either result or purpose; the certainty of the result is not the poet's concern so much as the harried ceaselessness of the struggle towards the result. He is deeply disturbed, too, although he says so only indirectly, by the frenzied handling of human lives. Both of these reactions are overwhelmed in the splendid final lines, which envisage the end of the rebirth cycle in an ecstasy of contemplative desire beside which belief would seem a trivial attitude. Reincarnation is important because of the human implications that can be attached to it. The poem envelops and transcends reincarnation as a belief by making it the only possible outlet for the speaker's thoughts and feelings.

By the early 'nineties Yeats had learned how to employ ideas in this larger context. He was delighted to discover hints of the rebirth cycle in ancient Irish legends, for it thus became part of the tradition of his own country and the west as well as of the east. . . . Fergus in the poem "Fergus and the Druid," from the

Countess Kathleen volume (1892), discovers through the druid's aid all the lives he has lived in the past:

> I see my life go dripping like a stream
> From change to change; I have been many things—
> A green drop in the surge, a gleam of light
> Upon a sword, a fir-tree on a hill,
> An old slave grinding at a heavy quern,
> A king sitting upon a chair of gold,
> And all these things were wonderful and great;
> But now I have grown nothing, being all,
> And the whole world weighs down upon my heart. . . .[3]

The theme, however, is not his discovery of past lives, but the pain which he experiences on surrendering his power as a king and man of action in return for even such spectacular knowledge. So doctrine is overshadowed here as well.

While it is conceivable that Yeats might have had outside his poems beliefs of a more obtrusive kind than those he put in his poems, he apparently did not. We have unusual evidence for his state of mind about reincarnation. The unpublished first draft of his *Autobiographies* recounts a conversation he had with Maud Gonne and George Russell in the middle 'nineties:

> He [Russell] had seen many visions, and some of them had contained information about matters of fact that were afterwards verified; but though his own personal revelations were often original and very remarkable, he accepted in the main the conclusions of Theosophy. He spoke of reincarnation and Maud Gonne asked him "how soon a child was reborn, and where." He said, "It may be reborn in the same family." I could see that Maud Gonne was deeply impressed and I quieted my more sceptical intelligence, as I had so often done in her presence. I remember a pang of conscience. Ought I not to say "The whole doctrine of the reincarnation of the soul is hypothetic; it is the most plausible of the explanations of the world, but can we say more than that?" or some such sentence?

This scruple is characteristic; although Yeats came to present the theme of reincarnation with a vehemence that increased with age and with the general strengthening of his mature verse, it was never more for him than the "most plausible of the explanations of the world." As such it stood him in good stead as a poet.

Reincarnation is closely related to a second concept in Yeats's verse. There, as in Eastern thought, the wheel of endless becoming

[3] For the final version of the poem, see *CP,* 32–33.

can be escaped and the soul transported to some kind of supreme existence which is changeless and immortal. This ideal state is neither exactly the Christian heaven nor the Buddhist Nirvana. Yeats invigorated and personalized it by giving it the irreligious names of "the happy townland," "the glittering town," and later on, "the predestined dancing-place" [*CP,* 82, 156]. A good deal of mystery surrounds this state: do we achieve it in this life, or must we bide our time until the afterlife? He took no permanent stand on this question, for to do so would have made him, like his friend Russell, a mystic given to unqualified assertion rather than a poet given to passionate longing. Russell's heaven was an abstraction, he thought, and he wrote his father in 1909: Russell "has set his ideal in so vague and remote a heaven that he takes the thoughts of his followers off the technique of life, or leaves only their poorer thoughts for it." He accepted instead J. B. Yeats's statement in a letter of 1914, "Poetry concerns itself with the creation of Paradises. I use the word in the plural for there are as many paradises as there are individual men—nay—as many as there are separate feelings." Heaven, then, is a name we apply to an ideal condition; whether it exists or not is of less importance than the fact that we demand its existence. What form we give it depends upon our feelings at a particular time.

Yeats's heaven is therefore startlingly variable. A comparison of the uncorrected and the corrected proof sheets of the "Apologia Addressed to Ireland in the Coming Days" (1892) reveals his determination to keep it so. The first version represents the perfect state as a union with truth which is attained only posthumously:

> From our birthday until we die,
> Is but the winking of an eye.
> And we, our singing and our love,
> The mariners of night above,
> And all the wizard things that go
> About my table to and fro,
> *Are passing on to where there is*
> *In truth's consuming silences*
> No place for love and dream at all;
> For God goes by with white footfall.[4]

The italicized lines contained two implications that Yeats felt obliged to alter. One was the dogmatic certainty of the state described, the other was the unpalatableness of even truth's

[4] For the final version, retitled "To Ireland in the Coming Times," see *CP,* 49–50.

transcending love and dream. He did not remove the lines, but he entered a significant qualification:

> Are passing on to where *may be*
> In truth's consuming ecstasy. . . .

Now his emphasis is not on the ideal state itself but on the possible peril to love and dream within it, and certainty or uncertainty are equally irrelevant.

The revision brings the poem closer to his statements in *The Shadowy Waters,* a play which elaborates his conceptions more lengthily than any other work in the 'nineties. Here the ideal state is the perfect union of hearts, not truth. Will the hero and heroine attain union in life or in death? Yeats admits the question without deciding it, preferring to celebrate the consummateness of their love,

> Whether among the cold winds of the dead,
> Or among winds that move in the meadows and woods.
> [*VP,* 768]

On the other hand, the wise man Dathi in "The Blessed" does not associate heaven only with love; he contends, too, that the state of blessedness can be reached in life in all sorts of ways, including drunkenness:

> O blessedness comes in the night and the day
> And whither the wise heart knows,
> And one has seen in the redness of wine
> The Incorruptible Rose. . . . [*CP,* 66]

Yeats was not required in his verse to side with a heaven attained through love, or a heaven attained through drunkenness, or to decide heaven's exact composition. He could admit as many paradises as separate ideals and longings. Yet the various heavens he describes have certain negative qualities in common: they are never thin, spiritualized, or fleshless. For a heaven that was purely spiritual seemed to him alien to poetry, which, he considered, must satisfy body as well as soul with its ideals. When in 1926 he came to write "Among School Children," he described his mature paradise consistently:

> Labour is blossoming or dancing where
> The body is not bruised to pleasure soul.

The location of "where" is left in doubt, but not the body's right to be the soul's peer in whatever heaven there may be.

A third theme, the approaching end of the world or its transmutation, is developed with the same constancy of attention and diversity of treatment. Several early poems picture a beast who will uproot the world in a consummation which sometimes appears to be the ultimate one, and at other times to be the upheaval heralding, in Theosophical doctrine, every new cycle. The beast, who invites comparison with the sphinx-like creature in "The Second Coming," which Yeats wrote in 1919, and with the donkey in *The Herne's Egg* (1938), is variously represented in the early poems as a grunting boar without bristles, a black pig, and a death-pale deer. While the first two, if not the third, are based on Irish folklore, the zoological variety is symptomatic of a variation in attitude. Sometimes Yeats diffidently heralds the approaching event; at other times he longs for it but sees no immediate prospect of its coming about; and elsewhere he half-regrets its coming. The eschatology is straightened or loosened to serve the particular poem and (to anticipate a little) the particular state of mind.

The introduction of religious imagery, especially of God or the gods, is a fourth problem of ideology in both Yeats's prose and verse. So much of this imagery is Christian that we might at first suppose that he attached religious significance to it. Mrs. Yeats has remarked that her husband prayed all his life; but if so it was not to any orthodox Christ. His attitude toward Christianity is complicated; like Blake he sometimes accepts Christ as divine because a symbol of imagination. So he wrote his friend William Horton in 1896, urging him to join the Golden Dawn on the grounds that this view of Christ was held by that society:

> Nor is our order anti-Christian. That very pentagram which I suggested your using is itself as you would presently have learned, a symbol of Christ. I am convinced however that for you progress lies not in dependence upon a Christ outside yourself but upon the Christ in your own breast, in the power of your divine will and divine imagination and not in some external will or imagination however divine. We certainly do teach this dependence only on the inner divinity but this is Christianity. The uttermost danger lies for you in emotional religion, which will sap your will and wreck your self-control. I do not mean that you cannot progress outside the G[olden] D[awn] but that you should read or study in some unemotional and difficult school. [*L*, 261–62]

Of course, as a poem on Father Rosicross [*CP*, 119] confirms,

Yeats would have accepted other symbols of the imagination just as readily as Christ.

Well before 1900, Yeats displays an increasing reluctance to employ Christ even as a symbol, for his birth and life seemed to him to be excessively spiritual. The hero of the unpublished novel, *The Speckled Bird,* proposes to improve Christianity by reconciling it with natural emotions and particularly with sexual love:

> . . . In Ireland he [found] wonderful doctrines among the poor, doctrines which would have been the foundation of the old Irish poets, and surely he would find somewhere in the East a doctrine that would reconcile religion with the natural emotions, and at the same time explain these emotions. All the arts sprang from sexual love and there they could only come again, the garb of the religion when that reconciliation had taken place.

In an article of 1897, Yeats argued that Irish Christianity was at its best when it had retained an infusion of paganism:

> Nothing shows more how blind educated Ireland—I am not certain that I should call so unimaginative a thing education—is about peasant Ireland, than that it does not understand how the old religion which made of the coming and going of the greenness of the woods and of the fruitfulness of the fields a part of its worship, lives side by side with the new religion which would trample nature as a serpent under its feet; nor is that old religion faded to a meaningless repetition of old customs, for the ecstatic who has seen the red light and white light of God smite themselves into the bread and wine at the Mass, has seen the exultant hidden multitudes among the winds of May, and if he were philosophical would cry with the painter, Calvert:—"I go inward to God, outward to the gods."

This point of view accorded with his other preoccupations, for he laboured to reunite nature and man by imaginative perception, and to evolve a poetry, with the force but without the constriction of religion, to educate humanity to an ampler life. His friend Russell suggested to him about this time that they build a chapel for fairy worship so that the Catholic worshippers might "become worshippers of the Sidhe without knowing it," a prospect which seemed to him as salutary as it was mischievous. He, like Yeats, wanted to break down the barriers in the interest of a higher unity.

When God appears in Yeats's verse, it is as an ultimate counter with which the imagination can round out its world. A good example is the morphology of a line in "He Remembers Forgotten Beauty." Yeats originally wrote:

> Where such grey clouds of incense rose
> That only God's eyes did not close;

then he altered the second line for a later edition, so that it read:

> That only the gods' eyes did not close;

and finally, for another edition, he restored the first version. The only motivation for this monotheism seems to be rhythm.

Elsewhere God is referred to as the "Eternal Darkness," "the Supreme Enchanter" (which makes his connection with the imagination especially close), the "Ineffable Name," "the Light of Lights," the "Master of the still stars and of the flaming door." In old age Yeats evolved more unusual terms still, like "the old man in the skies" and "the Thirteenth Cone."[5] He had cause for his ingenuity. No abstraction, as Blake had taught him, was more dangerous than a god abstracted from humanity, and frequent reference to divinity under conventional names seemed to him likely to erect just such an abstraction. Triteness could separate the poet from his object, and spiritual exaltation, even if not trite, could be poetically inapposite. Yeats wrote a shrewd letter in 1898 to Russell about the use of God. A tireless reviser of his friends' work as well as his own, he objected to a line in Russell's "Carrowmore" which read:

> Yet his sleep is filled with gold light by the King of all the world,

and explained, "I have changed 'King of all the world' which sounds a little commonplace to 'the masters of the world,' and 'gold light' which the verse puts out of the usual accentuation to 'music' which gives a full sound."[6] Russell meekly accepted the shift. Divinity might have a place in poetry, but not a prerogative. The poem, in short, came first.

Yeats's fixed policy was to shun the vast religious generalizations which were popular at the end of the nineteenth century. A year and a half before his death he had a talk with a

[5] *VP,* 688; *CP,* 49, 63, 307; *V,* 210, 301–2.

[6] Yeats followed his own advice in a poem, "The Players Ask for a Blessing on the Psalteries and on Themselves," where they address their prayer, or request, to the "masters of the glittering town." [Ellmann's note]

Hindu professor, to whom he asserted that he was no mystic. While he always took the westerner's part when talking to anyone from the East, just as in writing for a western audience he habitually introduced eastern conceptions, he was not speaking merely *ad hoc.* "In my own poetry," he said, "I have always aimed at perfect clearness of conception and a perfectly logical expression. Tagore, who is of course a great personal friend of mine, writes a great deal about God. My mind resents the vagueness of all references to God. I keep to what is clear and rational. . . . In my poetry there is always a clear conception expressed in language as perfect as I command." It is, in fact, true that God in Yeats's writings is either a poetic property like destiny, filling out the picture of the cosmos by providing it with leadership, or a symbol of some imaginative power, or imagined state of being, closely associated with man, and that in neither capacity is He likely to be described with vagueness. A very early poem, "The Indian upon God," is an excellent illustration. The Indian hears a moorfowl assert that God is "an undying moorfowl," a lotus protest that "He hangeth on a stalk," a roebuck that "He is a gentle roebuck," and a peacock that "He is a monstrous peacock." The poem would be equally congenial to Hume and Madame Blavatsky. Hume would say that it meant that all religions were founded on personal prejudice and therefore were false, and Madame Blavatsky would interpret it to mean that all religions, whatever their particular forms, sprang from a common and valid instinct. Yeats would say that he had not written the poem to express either of these dogmas, and that neither inference was an adequate restatement. Primarily the poem meant to him that these creatures were right in imagining their God as like themselves, concrete and personal, while man was wrong when he tried to create his God out of some other substance than humanity.

The essential standard for the poet is one of "dwelling in the presence of certain ideas" rather than of positing them as truths demanding adherence; he relies on the complexity of poetic structure to prevent his verse from being doctrinal. The references to God in most of the early poems are alike in exhibiting no affection for Him and not much attention to His present power in the world. Rather Yeats summons Him from the sky to destroy or transmute the world in the near future, and so concentrates on the attitudes of fear and hope rather than of piety. This treatment is not atheism, but it should not be mistaken for orthodoxy or devotion either. Far from being a

God-intoxicated man, Yeats has only to think of God to become sober and extremely wary.

Instead of worshipping an abstraction, Yeats advocates, in one of his short stories, the "unfolding" of the individual's heart. This personal ethic, which he opposes to conventional ethics, is the fifth recurrent idea in his verse. Critics have sometimes identified him with a doctrine of art for art's sake, and so misinterpreted him. Like his father, Yeats was disinclined to discuss ethical questions theoretically; he had had enough of the emphasis on conduct in nineteenth-century letters. At the age of twenty, in some notes about George Eliot, he irritably announced: "There is too much talk of the moral law, surely the tongue of the poet is for other teaching. Is there not a pulpited million of disconsolate voices shouting the moral law for so much a day?" Sometimes he impatiently opposed morals altogether, sometimes he simply indicated his satiety with them, and sometimes he reconstituted them.

His fundamental position was that good and bad in their usual senses were, as Blake had said, nets of convention. The writer, and any man of personality, must steer clear of them. As he put it in *The Celtic Twilight* (1893), fantasy and caprice would lose their necessary freedom if united either with evil or good. The hero of "The Tables of the Law" is incapable of sin, because he "had discovered the law of my being, and could only express or fail to express my being" [*M,* 305]. If one must have sins, they should be one's own and no one else's; in a lecture in 1909, Yeats spoke of "the old writers as busy with their own sins and of the new writers as busy with other people's," ranking Shakespeare on one side and Milton on the other. He had said in his edition of Blake that truth is "the dramatic expression of the most complete man," and the same definition would have served for his notion of good.

In youth as in old age, he was struggling to be rid of stereotyped ethical judgments. . . . The self has the task of expressing itself, but it can be judged by its own completeness, and by the completeness of its expression. It has to be able to respect itself, and to do so tries to live up to some image of desirable life. The hero at Mount Meru, or Troy, or the Dublin Post Office, the poet at his desk framing the most complex experiences, and the young girl in the indolence of her youth have other things to be concerned with than the tables of abstract law. Their self-imposed ideals of conduct, through which they aspire to completeness, possess their thoughts.

III. SYMBOLIST THEORY

The centre of a Yeats poem is not its ideological content. It is rather, Yeats said as a young man, a mood, or as he later put it, a state of mind. He meant both terms to be large enough to include both emotions and ideas. Moods and states of mind are conspicuously, but not exclusively, emotional or temperamental; they differ from emotions in having form and, often, intellectual structure. Less fleeting than a mere wish, and less crystallized than a belief, a mood is suspended between fluidity and solidity. It can be tested only by the likelihood of its being experienced at all, and being so, by many people. Ideas which occur in moods are "lived" and lose their abstractness; beliefs are dramatized and lose their affiliations with dogmas to take on affiliations with the dramatic speaker of the poem.

Moods are not aroused by the rational faculty or by "undisciplined squads of emotion," but by the imagination, which has both at its disposal. If, for example, the reason tells us that the reality we see is the only reality, the imagination may contradict it, affirming that the corporeal eye is only an instrument and not a very important one. More important than that eye is our dreaming or visionary faculty, which is second-sighted and conceives a reality more fundamental than Zola's. Of dreams, visions, folklore, and works of art, Yeats writes in the *National Observer,* "They are an existence and not a thought, and make our world of the tea-tables seem but a shabby penumbra."

No reader would be so brazen as to defend the reality of tea-tables, yet one might object that the poet exploits this scorn to justify discarding the world of appearance altogether. He does not go so far, however. His fondness for words like dream, ideal, phantasy, symbol, delusion, glamour, and image permits him to "exchange civilities with the world beyond"; to carry it further would be to isolate one part of the mind from the rest.

By keeping up a running battle with the world of appearance, Yeats gives it covert recognition. As early as 1893, he writes in *The Celtic Twilight,* "I too had by this time fallen into a kind of trance, in which what we call the unreal had begun to take upon itself a masterful reality. . . . Everything exists, everything is true, and the earth is only a little dust under our feet." Sometimes he transvaluates the word "dream" so that the world of appearance is the dream, and the *au-delà* is the reality, as when Niamh invites mortals to "Empty your heart of its mortal dream" [*CP,* 53]. But "dream" may also have its more conventional meaning, as in "The Song of the Last Arcadian," where the poet urges, "Dream, dream, for this is also sooth" [*CP,* 8]. These statements do not offer philosophical distinctions between appearance and reality, but tensions between them; while either term is likely to shift its meaning, Yeats regularly exalts all that is imagined and denigrates all that is seen if it falls short of what is imagined. He well knew Blake's declaration that to him the sun was not a round disc of fire somewhat like a guinea but an innumerable company of the heavenly host crying, "Holy, holy, holy is the Lord God Almighty." But Yeats did not wish to deprive the moods of their ties with common perception, only to free them from absolute dependence on those ties.

In the same way, he freed them from dependence on rational foundations. "It is better doubtless," he wrote winningly, "to believe much unreason and a little truth than to deny for denial's sake truth and unreason alike. . . . When all is said and done, how do we not know but that our own unreason may be better than another's truth?" [*The Celtic Twilight*]. The tortured syntax may well put a hard-headed reader on Yeats's side, and lead him to ignore the fact that all denial is not for denial's sake. Yeats was not necessarily so elliptical. Speaking to the Irish Literary Society in London, he asserted that there were truths of passion which were intellectual falsehoods; in many of his writings he insisted that the peasant knew and revealed more in his folklore than the metropolitan in his technical books. "Folk-lore," he announced, "is at once the Bible, the Thirty-Nine Articles, and the Book of Common Prayer, and well-nigh all the great poets have lived by its light. Homer, Aeschylus, Sophocles, Shakespeare, and even Dante, Goethe, and Keats, were little more than folk-lorists with musical tongues" [*Speaker,* 8 (August 1893)]. The respect for folklore, as for passion, was to rob the intellect of ascendancy.

Since the moods are informed by the imagination, they are the most real things or beings we know. "The great Moods are alone immortal, and the creators of mortal things," Yeats reverently declares in *The Secret Rose.* How they appear to us, or better, befall us, he describes in "Rosa Alchemica":

> For just as the magician or the artist could call them when he would, so they could call out of the mind of the magician or the artist, or if they were demons, out of the mind of the mad or the ignoble, what shape they would, and through its voice and its gestures pour themselves out upon the world. In this way all great events were accomplished; a mood, a divinity or a demon, first descending like a faint sigh into men's minds and then changing

> their thoughts and their actions until hair that was yellow had grown black, or hair that was black had grown yellow, and empires moved their border, as though they were but drifts of leaves. [*M,* 285–86]

They offer a sanction for the "monumental moments" of dramatic lyrics, for at bottom, Yeats explained in an important essay in 1895, art has no content but moods:

> Literature differs from explanatory and scientific writing in being wrought about a mood, or a community of moods, as the body is wrought about an invisible soul; and if it uses argument, theory, erudition, observation, and seems to grow hot in assertion or denial, it does so merely to make us partakers at the banquet of the moods. It seems to me that . . . argument, theory, erudition, observation, are merely what Blake called "little devils who fight for themselves," illusions of our visible passing life, who must be made serve the moods, or we have no part in eternity. Everything that can be seen, touched, measured, explained, understood, argued over, is to the imaginative artist nothing more than a means. . . . [*E&I,* 195]

Beyond the moods there is no more ultimate reality, unless it is their union. In his edition of Blake, Yeats, having pointed out the divergencies of different mystical systems, justified them as expressions of moods:

> Sometimes the mystical student, bewildered by the different systems, forgets for a moment that the history of moods is the history of the universe, and asks where is the final statement—the complete doctrine. The universe is itself that doctrine and statement. All others are partial, for it alone is the symbol of the infinite thought which is in turn symbolic of the universal mood we name God.

It is characteristic of his point of view that the final "doctrine and statement" turns out to have no formulation except that of the universe which is itself a symbol. It is the symbol of God, Himself a symbol of "the universal mood," the *prima materia.* Mood is piled on mood to such an extent that everything is symbolically related, and we can define any given mood only by establishing precisely its correspondence with others. So considered, heaven, hell, purgatory, and fairyland may be simply names attributed to certain moods; thus hell is "the place of those who deny" its existence.[7]

[7] In the play *The Hour-Glass.*

Whether the human imagination creates moods, or only evokes them, was a question that Yeats asked himself. Sometimes he took the solipsist position. So in some notes for his unpublished novel, *The Speckled Bird,* he went as far as he could: "The Rosicrucian magic means the assertion of the greatness of man in its extreme form. His [the hero's] letter should give some eloquent expression to this. He may even claim with the Druids that man created the world." A quarter of a century later Yeats made this claim in "The Tower":

> Death and life were not
> Till man made up the whole,
> Made lock, stock and barrel
> Out of his bitter soul,
> Aye, sun and moon and star, all,
> And further add to that
> That, being dead, we rise,
> Dream and so create
> Translunar Paradise. [*CP,* 196]

Yet if such a claim had complete pre-eminence over all others, it would have contradicted his conception of poetry as an assemblage of moods. He justifiably did not base all his poems on the solipsist theory.

The value of the moods to his poetry was threefold. First, they exempted it from the powerful conscriptive pressure of conventional beliefs and fashionable doubts; they made imagination, whether the breeding-house or the nursery of moods, more important than reason and more permanent than emotion. "Whatever we build in the imagination," he wrote Florence Farr in 1899, "will accomplish itself in the circumstance of our lives." Second, they unified the world into one imaginative substance; they replaced the *matter* of the scientists with the *mood* of the poets. Third, they made forceful asseveration possible to a man whose point of view was flexible. They admitted the poet to a world which the scientist, the banker, the clergyman, and the philosopher, clutching like dolls their substitute-realities, were forbidden to enter.

Denis Donoghue

The Human Image in Yeats

Yeats: a poet intensely and often painfully preoccupied with the irreconcilable claims of Soul and Body; "body and soul/ Estranged amid the strangeness of themselves" [*CP,* 162]. Intensely and painfully, because being a poet he was driven toward images of "wholeness," unity, and "perfection." It seemed impossible to realize "Unity of Being," that state in which "all the nature murmurs in response if but a single note be touched." Indeed, by the time he came to write the second Book of *The Trembling of the Veil,* he had modified that demand. I now know, he said, "that there are men who cannot possess 'Unity of Being,' who must not seek it or express it. . . . They must await that which lies beyond their mind . . . the man of science, the moralist, the humanitarian, the politician. . . ." In "King and no King" he had written:

> And I that have not your faith, how shall I know
> That in the blinding light beyond the grave,
> We'll find so good a thing as that we have lost?
> The hourly kindness, the day's common speech,
> The habitual content of each with each
> When neither soul nor body has been crossed.

There were many moments in which Yeats thought—or hoped against hope—that everything would be fulfilled in the

From The Ordinary Universe: Soundings in Modern Literature *by Denis Donoghue (The Macmillan Company, New York, 1968), pp. 108–122, 139, 141–144, 310–311.* *Copyright © by Denis Donoghue.* *And from* An Honored Guest: New Essays on W. B. Yeats, *edited by Denis Donoghue and J. R. Mulryne (St. Martin's Press, New York, 1966), pp. 115, 120.* *Copyright © 1965 by Edward Arnold (publishers), Ltd. Extracts from both volumes reprinted by permission of A. D. Peters and Company.*

accords of a distinguished human body; that the body, in splendid animation, would certify an undissociated unity of being, like the transfiguration which Ribh conjured at the tomb of Baile and Ailinn [*CP*, 282]. Yeats often recited harmonious parables like "The Three Bushes"; and perhaps he was drawn toward the alchemists because their object was—in Jung's summary—"to produce a *corpus subtile*, a transfigured and resurrected body, i.e. a body that was at the same time spirit."[1] This would relate his meditations upon unknown thought to the woman Homer sang and both to whatever "unconditioned" state was his God-term for the time being. But more soberly he named the body a dissociated and dying animal [see *CP*, 191].

This is Yeats as patient. As agent he sought to heal himself: first, by lamenting the lost harmony, invoking a great-rooted chestnut tree that suffered from none of man's dissociations. And again: with a dramatist's instinct he broke down the crux into its two conflicting parts; thereafter interpreting experience, as his "condition" prodded, now in terms of Soul (or Spirit), now in terms of Body (or Nature). The crux was a complex and unmanageable simultaneity: Yeats replaced it, imperatively, by a more tolerable scheme of successiveness. He resolved a contradictory "yes-no" situation by setting up a plot that developed from "yes" to "no" and vice versa.[2]

In *The Wanderings of Oisin, Crossways, The Rose,* and *The Wind among the Reeds* Yeats located the Spirit in a realm of picturesque sorrow with "numberless islands," "many a Danaan shore," and a "woven world-forgotten isle." In those books whatever mode of existence is identified with the Spirit is protected from the critique of Body or Nature. Those early poems are a long and intermittently beautiful "yes" to the Spirit; but the Spirit is abused, maimed, because torn from the Body. In later years and with different materials Yeats often said "yes" to the Spirit; under the guise of Mind, for instance, as in "All Souls' Night":

> Such thought—such thought have I that hold it tight
> Till meditation master all its parts,
> Nothing can stay my glance
> Until that glance run in the world's despite
> To where the damned have howled away their hearts,
> And where the blessed dance;

[1] Carl Jung, *Psychology and Alchemy;* translated by R. F. C. Hull (London, Routledge and Kegan Paul, 1953), p. 408. [Donoghue's note]

[2] Cf. Kenneth Burke, "Mysticism as a Solution of the Poet's Dilemma:" in Stanley Romaine Hopper (editor), *Spiritual Problems in Contemporary Literature* (New York, Harper, 1952), pp. 95 f. [Donoghue's note]

HIGHLAND COMMUNITY
JUNIOR COLLEGE LIBRARY
HIGHLAND, KANSAS

Such thought, that in it bound
I need no other thing,
Wound in mind's wandering
As mummies in the mummy-cloth are wound.

In this poem Yeats praises those adepts who, like Florence Emery, meditate upon unknown thought and repudiate the Body:

What matter who it be,
So that his elements have grown so fine
The fume of muscatel
Can give his sharpened palate ecstacy
No living man can drink from the whole wine.

Ours are "gross palates." This is one situation, one act in the plot. Its counterpart is the Crazy Jane series in *Words for Music Perhaps.*

The year is 1929. Yeats is recovering from an attack of Maltese fever. Behind him, or so he fancies, are the world of politics, the Irish Senate, and "a sixty-year-old smiling public man." He writes to Olivia Shakespear from Rapallo: "No more opinions, no more politics, no more practical tasks" [*L,* 761]. Joyful riddance: it is a prosperous moment. Sixty-four years old, Yeats feels new strength and sexual energy returning to his body. He is impelled to have recourse to that "nature" (in bodily terms) from which he had withdrawn, estranged, to a more gracious world of pure Mind. Now he withdraws again, provisionally, not only from pure Mind but from a "practical" scene of disillusion. Ridding himself of a practical world he reduces his scene accordingly: he identifies his will, provisionally, with the urges of the body in revolt, giving it—for protection and definition—the name "Crazy Jane."

It is a simplification on Yeats's part, and therefore an evasion. Indeed, each of Yeats's books of poems is a strategic simplification, a trial account of his universe devoted not to the entire complex truth but to a particular bias which is dominant for the time being. Some are phoenix books; others, turtle books; what one longs for is the mutual flame:

Hearts remote, yet not asunder;
Distance, and no space was seen.[3]

In the Crazy Jane poems Yeats for the time being places as much

[3] These lines, and "mutual flame," are, of course, from Shakespeare's "Phoenix and the Turtle."

trust in the bodily (a turtle, surely) as Racine in the greatly passionate, or Wordsworth in the greatly sensitive. The bodily imperative is the "myth" of the Crazy Jane poems, corresponding to the anthropological myth of "The Waste Land."

Words for Music Perhaps; the words are for music, not because they are to be sung, but because their burden, like that of the ballad, belongs to the folk. The context has "the body's potencies"—Lawrence's phrase—as its prime motive.

The connotations are important. It is "that foul body" in "Those Dancing Days are Gone," but this does not mean—as a recent critic maintains—that Yeats "identifies the physical, corporcal aspects of love with that which is foul," or that in his later poems, going one better, he "regards the sexual act as mostly beastly." Quite the opposite. There is a curious tone in those Crazy Jane poems:

> Come, let me sing into your ear;
> Those dancing days are gone,
> All that silk and satin gear;
> Crouch upon a stone,
> Wrapping that foul body up
> In as foul a rag: [*CP,* 261]

The body is not foul. What is foul—here—is its decay, its loss of power, mainly sexual ("the vigour of its blood"). Six days before writing this poem Yeats had rendered that bodily power in "Crazy Jane Grown Old Looks at the Dancers":

> God be with the times when I
> Cared not a thraneen for what chanced
> So that I had the limbs to try
> Such a dance as there was danced—
> *Love is like the lion's tooth.*

Again in "Mad as the Mist and Snow" the winds are foul because they testify to decay. In "All Souls' Night" the years are foul because they wear away Florence Emery's beauty. Indeed, Yeats uses the word when he has in mind sheer mutability. A difficult case is "Crazy Jane Talks with the Bishop:"

> I met the Bishop on the road
> And much said he and I.
> 'Those breasts are flat and fallen now,
> Those veins must soon be dry;
> Live in a heavenly mansion,
> Not in some foul sty.'

The choice is offered as if it were unanswerable; the Bishop, as rhetorician, has no time for the Gidean problematic. Here, of course, "foul" is censorial, and we expect the Bishop to be whipped for his cliché. Crazy Jane accepts the word and its challenge:

> 'Fair and foul are near of kin,
> And fair needs foul,' I cried.

There is also, she claims, the God of Love; and he has rights, a trim decorum, and his own special mansion. And the term[s] he proffers—since two can play the rhetorical game—have a sanction prior to that of the Bishop's God, because they are certified by the axioms of the body and by "the heart's pride":

> 'A woman can be proud and stiff
> When on love intent;
> But Love has pitched his mansion in
> The place of excrement;
> For nothing can be sole or whole
> That has not been rent.'

A devotee of Blake, she has the last word.[4]

She has the first word in "Crazy Jane on the Day of Judgement," and here her interpretation of love has a wider circumference than usual. Indeed the Crazy Jane of this poem encompasses the three great dramatic roles through which, as Richard Ellmann has observed, Yeats voiced his conceptions. First, she is the Seer:

> 'Love is all
> Unsatisfied
> That cannot take the whole
> Body and soul';

the Victim:

> 'Naked I lay,
> The grass my bed;
> Naked and hidden away,
> That black day';

[4] Crazy Jane's conclusion recalls a line from Blake's *Jerusalem:* "For I will make their places of Joy and love excrementitious." Jane, the greatest Yeatsian Fool, also embodies Blake's proverb of Hell: "If the fool would persist in his folly he would become wise."

finally, the Assessor:

> 'What can be shown?
> What true love be?
> All could be known or shown
> If Time were but gone.'

The poem is intensely moving because it is willing to test the possibilities of growth and extension in a conception of love based on the bodily imperative. Crazy Jane's speculations do not go very far, and anything like an Incarnational view of the body is as far removed from her as from Yeats himself at any point; but in this poem there is an urge to face radical questions which are often evaded in *Words for Music Perhaps.* This book is devoted to a partial view of things: Crazy Jane has a deeper idea of love than Jack the Journeyman, but she is less urgently engaged in refining this idea than in knocking down Aunt Sallies like the Bishop. In the later "Supernatural Songs" Ribh plays a similar role; not so much enacting the whole as insisting upon the part which, he asserts, the Christian view discards; "the phallic consciousness," again Lawrence's phrase:

> Natural and supernatural with the self-same ring are wed.
> As man, as beast, as an ephemeral fly begets, Godhead
> begets Godhead,
> For things below are copies, the Great Smaragdine Tablet
> said. [*CP*,283]

Crazy Jane and Ribh are propagandists, speaking half-truths by vocation. They may be more humanely "right" than the Bishop, but they are just as severely dissociated as he, and the poetic metaphor is just as far beyond their grasp. If the speaker in "All Souls' Night" is a Paleface, Crazy Jane and Ribh are Redskins—to use Philip Rahv's famous terms; countering the "sensibility" of *The Tower* with their own "experience." But the experience is raw, and therefore equally vulnerable to irony.

Yeats wanted his "Poems for Music" to be "all emotion and all impersonal." On 2nd March 1929—the day on which he wrote "Crazy Jane and the Bishop" and "Crazy Jane Grown Old Looks at the Dancers"—he referred to the poems: "They are the opposite of my recent work and all praise of joyous life, though in the best of them it is a dry bone on the shore that sings the praise" [*L,* 758]. Joyous life in this book is life in which the prime commitment is to the body. Everything else may change or be dissolved, but not that.

Until now we have been discussing the book as Yeats's "self-expression." But it is necessary to add another context, involving the persuasive relation between the poet and his audience.

Yeats "believed in" none of the public, institutional faiths. But he needed their authority, their momentum, or at least authority and momentum from similar sources. And he was a spectacular rhetorician. So he used each of the public faiths whenever he felt that one of its patterns of insight was specially relevant to the feeling of the poem. He may have been drawn to these local "allegiances" by sensing a purely formal congruity between the pattern in the "public" structure and the pattern implicit in the private feeling. This would account for the Way of the Cross in "The Travail of Passion," to certify feeling akin to its own; or the figure of the Guardian Angel in "A Prayer for My Son." Similarly in the Crazy Jane poems the bodily imperative is a "public" pattern of experience, with the force of public authority, complete with dogmas, rites, mysteries—and these by universal assent. The great advantage of the bodily imperative as a source of verbal communication is that it is prior to all conflicts of thought or belief; it under-cuts the contentious levels of experience. In lofty moments Yeats would invoke the Great Memory as the source and means of communication, and he would speak beautifully under its sign, but there would always be something problematic in its operation. The human body was more reliable; indeed, the body was the only universal Church to which Yeats would belong.

We have described a strategic simplification and called it—harshly—evasion. And we would suggest that a great mind which has recourse to such a strategy must harbour severe misgivings, knowing that it omits so much, condones so much distortion. That is why one has the feeling, reading the later books, that very often Yeats is adopting certain roles not to protect himself from tourists but because he fancies himself in the parts; like the "character part" of the lusty old man or the ruthless neo-Fascist. A new and distressing kind of picturesque, this leads to a certain hardening of the arteries in such a poem as "News for the Delphic Oracle." Here is part of the first stanza:

> Man-picker Niamh leant and sighed
> By Oisin on the grass;
> There sighed amid his choir of love
> Tall Pythagoras.

Porphyry's Elysian Fields are very like Yeats's Islands of Forgetfulness, and Yeats—sly old virtuoso—can now jeer at both. With the same virtuosity he can laugh at the equestrian Innocents:

> Straddling each a dolphin's back
> And steadied by a fin,
> Those Innocents re-live their death,
> Their wounds open again.

The last word is Yeats's: he offers it, surely, as critique:

> Foul goat-head, brutal arm appear,
> Belly, shoulder, bum,
> Flash fishlike; nymphs and satyrs
> Copulate in the foam.

Touché. Yes, but isn't it, itself, in a weak position, despite the bodily imperative and the sophisticated accent? The poem has ended, but one could envisage a fourth stanza (by Dante) in which the Old-Yeatsian heaven of the third would be shown for the vulnerable thing it is. The critique is valid enough as far as it goes, but not valid enough to justify the tone, the shrill exhibitionist mockery. The Yeats of the *Last Poems* did not often laugh in the tragic joy of Lear and Hamlet; his laughter is too shrill for that. The apocalypse of these poems is a willed tumult, the poet goading himself into the role of a randy old man to repel the temptations of a laureate old age. (But there are great humane exceptions to this rule, such as "The Circus Animals' Desertion," "An Acre of Grass," and "Beautiful Lofty Things.")

This shrillness in Yeats's late work issues, I think, from those misgivings which I have mentioned. In *Words for Music Perhaps, A Full Moon in March,* and many of the *Last Poems* Yeats's strategic simplifications landed him in a false position; hence the strident tone.

He soon got tired of Crazy Jane, though, perhaps acknowledging the limited range of her insight. He used her once again, innocuously, cursing puny times and a world bereft of Cuchulains [in "Crazy Jane on the Mountain," *CP,* 335].

Words for Music Perhaps—a final comment before we look at other human images in Yeats—is a valuable book because it enables us to re-enact a movement of feeling downward into the limited, finite thing. The movement is touching in itself, in its compulsions and embarrassments; only the most sullen reader could fail to be moved and disturbed by this partial image of the human condition. The pathos of the book is that when Yeats had reached down into the finite Body there was little he could do with it; he saw no means of penetrating the finite without transcending it and thereby destroying it, as Roderick destroyed Madeline, in a rage for essence.[5] The trouble was that he could not value the human body in itself; only when it agreed to wear a bright halo of animation.

It is painful dialectic. The poet for whom plenitude of being is everything finds himself kicking several of man's faculties out of the way in his rage for essence. The devotee of "perfection" bows before fragments. In his most perceptive moments he knows that it is a desperate expedient, that even his Byzantine eternity is artifice:

> It seems that I must bid the Muse go pack,
> Choose Plato and Plotinus for a friend
> Until imagination, ear and eye,
> Can be content with argument and deal
> In abstract things; or be derided by
> A sort of battered kettle at the heel. ["The Tower," *CP,* 192]

If you reduce a human being to his consciousness, and then provide a diet of unknown thought, argument, and abstraction, you must face the risks involved; attrition, emaciation, a desert of mummies. Time and again in *The Tower* Yeats prays for a kinder unity:

> O may the moon and sunlight seem
> One inextricable beam,
> For if I triumph I must make men mad. [*CP,* 193–94]

But that book is a little too engrossed with its own exposure to allow much consideration for other people; apart from a few chosen friends, the rest are given as hot-faced bargainers and money-changers. And what can we say of the monstrous crudity, the sheer vulgarity, of "Mrs. French,/Gifted with so fine an ear"? Grant that Yeats's position was difficult, perhaps impossible. "All Souls' Night" was written under the sign of body-wearied Plotinus; as in the fourth *Ennead,* the dying animal of "Sailing to Byzantium" is here dead, a mummy, and the "soul" moves from its prison of diminished being. But in Yeats it has nowhere to go; the poet could

[5] In Poe's "The Fall of the House of Usher."

not make anything of Plotinus's belief in the later stages of emanation toward the One. Hence the desperate stratagem, six years later, of "Byzantium."

"All Souls' Night" is almost a test case for the hazard of the human image. It is a thrilling poem; we are at once thrilled and shocked to find Yeats driving himself into such a terrifying corner. The position itself—we feel at once—is untenable. It is unnecessarily dissociative. Mind—as Philip Wheelwright puts it—"does not stand alone: it exists intentively in relation to objects and it exists dialogically in relation to other selves."[6] So the intensity of "All Souls' Night" amounts to this: a stern mind denying the most serviceable relations in a humane life, and holding this denial "to the end of the line." If intensity were enough, this poem, this action, would be one of the greatest achievements in modern literature, and we would assent to it without reservation and find in it none of the wilfulness which disturbs us now. But intensity is not enough, and may well serve no other purpose than to assure us that we exist.

Does this matter? Or is it the fury in the words that matters, and not the words?

The received opinion among readers of Yeats is that the classic poems are in *The Tower.* And yet by comparison with *The Wild Swans at Coole* the human image in that spectacular book is curiously incomplete; remarkably intense, but marginal; a little off-centre. Does this matter? Yes, it does; intensity is not enough. It matters greatly that *The Wild Swans at Coole* is at the very heart of the human predicament, groping for values through which man may define himself without frenzy or servility.

This book is concerned with the behaviour of men in the cold light of age and approaching death. The ideal stance involves passion, self-conquest, courtesy, and moral responsibility. Yeats pays the tribute of wild tears to many people and to the moral beauty which they embody; the entire book is rammed with moral life. Most of the poems were written between 1915 and 1919, and it is significant that those were the years in which Yeats was perfecting his dance-drama; because the dancer was the culmination of the efforts which Yeats made in *The Wild Swans at Coole* to represent the fullness of being as a dynamic action. Frank Kermode in his *Romantic Image* has discussed the role of the dance, in Yeats's poems, as the embodiment of that image, and more recently he has suggested the kind of dancer Yeats had in mind. We know from *The Death of Cuchulain* that it was not the

[6] Philip Wheelwright, "The Intellectual Light," *Sewanee Review,* LXVI, 3, Summer, 1958, p. 411. [Donoghue's note]

dancer painted by Degas; their chambermaid faces distressed him when he wanted something "timeless"; and clearly their glamour was a little low for his taste. Loie Fuller's dancing, Mr. Kermode argues, had precisely the connotations Yeats demanded: "She is abstract, clear of the human mess, dead, and yet perfect being, as on some Byzantine floor: entirely independent of normal action, out of time."[7] It is beyond dispute that Yeats and many of his artistic contemporaries were fascinated by this dancer; and yet the description does not seem quite in keeping with the dance-climaxes of Yeats's own later plays, which do not try to evade time at all. The Yeatsian dance seems much more severe, much stricter than the Symbolist dance of Loie Fuller. We should recall the description of the ideal dancer which the Old Man provides in *The Death of Cuchulain:* "The tragi-comedian dancer, the tragic dancer, upon the same neck love and loathing, life and death." This is much more Yeatsian, I think, than the dancer of Mr. Kermode's description. It is also much more in keeping with the human image of *The Wild Swans at Coole,* which has nothing in common with the bodiless, timeless vision of Loie Fuller. It would seem very strange if Yeats, after *The Green Helmet,* were to present fullness of being in an image itself timeless and bodiless. Indeed, the dance was a powerful image precisely because it was committed to body; an apt equivalent in our own time is the dance-drama of Merce Cunningham or Martha Graham, which glories in the physicality of the body, in its muscular and nervous experience, in the resistance of the ground itself. Yeats's dancer is never allowed to circumvent the body or to grow wings.

In "The Double Vision of Michael Robartes" the girl who dances between the Sphinx and the Buddha dreams of dancing and has outdanced thought; which I take to mean that in her Action is not distinct from Vision but is Vision itself formulated. The moral equivalent of this is a certain nonchalance or recklessness, Castiglione's *sprezzatura,* a certain high daring; mastery, rather than singularity, to cite Valéry's distinction. As a gloss we may quote a few sentences from Buber's meditations upon Nijinsky:

"The decisive power in the development of the dance was neither play nor expression, but what bound them and gave them law: magic. That is the response to the chaotic and furiously in-

[7] Poet and Dancer before Diaghilev," *Partisan Review,* XXVIII, I, January–February 1961, p. 75. [Donoghue's note]

rushing happening through the bound, lawful movement, through movement as form. The bound binds."[8]

Above all, it must be dynamic, this ideal behaviour; it must not be complacently picturesque. In T. S. Eliot's later poems this ideal condition appears a little static; the poet may say, "at the still point, there the dance is," but there is very little energy in that dance, and we have to exert some goodwill before we can register it at all. In some of Wallace Stevens's poems the ideal condition is given as a still life—a blue woman, in August, registering grape leaves and clouds—someone sitting in a park watching the archaic form of a woman with a cloud on her shoulder. These are handsome moments, and we are free to relish them. But Yeats knew that they are at best provisional, at worst evasive; in his greatest poems static effects denote a failure of being.

The Wild Swans at Coole is committed to action; not to thought or concept or feeling, except that these are essential to the full definition of action. We are to register action as the most scrupulous notation of human existence, far more accurate, more "creatural," than thought or concept—which are simplifications; far more comprehensive, too. Action is silent articulation of experience. Yeats's dancer has outdanced thought, summarized thought in a pattern of gestures. Her dance is an act of desire toward the God-state, or God-term; the dancer strives toward an "essential" human image, an image of dynamic perfection freely formulated—fulfilled—at the end of the body-line. This is probably what Yeats meant in the well-known letter which he wrote a few weeks before his death, in which he said, "It seems to me that I have found what I wanted. When I try to put all into a phrase, I say, 'Man can embody truth but he cannot know it' " [*L*, 922]. Truth is embodied in the figure of action, the dancer for whom meaning is embodied in gesture and gesture the only expression there is. Thought is not enough; even the "thinking of the body": the most accurate annotation is that act which outdances thought and sums up human potentiality in gesture.

In *The Wild Swans at Coole* the dance which engrosses Yeats is the dance of the self and anti-self. In "Ego Dominus Tuus" the Yeatsian speaker says:

> I call to the mysterious one who yet
> Shall walk the wet sands by the edge of the stream
> And look most like me, being indeed my double,

[8] Martin Buber, *Pointing the Way,* translated by Maurice Friedman (New York, Harper, 1957), p. 23. [Donoghue's note]

And prove of all imaginable things
The most unlike, being my anti-self
And, standing by these characters, disclose
All that I seek. . . .

The appropriate gloss is from "Anima Hominis": "Unlike the rhetoricians, who get a confident voice from remembering the crowd they have won or may win, we sing amid our uncertainty; and, smitten even in the presence of the most high beauty by the knowledge of our solitude, our rhythm shudders" [*M,* 331]. Add to this that Art is a vision of reality [*CP,* 159]: in the artist this vision is animated by his own passion, and in the passion his rhythm shudders. This is the dance, the ecstasy, man and daimon feeding the hunger in one another's hearts.

It is also dialogue, the fruitful grappling of self and anti-self. Hence the number of poems in *The Wild Swans at Coole* in which the structure is "dialogical" and the animation is the rhythm of speech. One of the finest examples is "The People":

'What have I earned for all that work,' I said
'For all that I have done at my own charge?
The daily spite of this unmannerly town,
Where who has served the most is most defamed,
The reputation of his lifetime lost
Between the night and morning. I might have lived,
And you know well how great the longing has been,
Where every day my footfall should have lit
In the green shadow of Ferrara wall.'. . .

This is the mutual flame. A poet, in weariness, voices a natural demand, claims the reward of the rhetorician; quarrelling with others, he makes a rhetoric, strong if a little sullen. He is in the condition of earth, the "place of heterogeneous things," as Yeats calls it, and he is admonished by his phoenix, the spirit of fire "that makes all simple." The common ground between them is the human world, which includes Castiglione's aristocrats[9] as well as "the people." The poet prolongs the dispute by setting up a conflict between the purity of a natural force and the definitions of the analytic mind; but the dispute is helpless. The real dispute, the real dialogue, is under the words, in the meeting of phoenix and turtle, the leaping of his heart at her words, the sinking of his head abashed. This is the poet's quarrel with himself. If we

[9] Yeats was significantly influenced by Castiglione's *Book of the Courtier.* See Corinna Salvadori, *Yeats and Castiglioni, Poet and Courtier,* Barnes & Noble, New York, 1965.

feel that the proper response to this poem is intimacy and assent, the reason is clear: the poem commits itself to the human situation, to the specific occasion of dialogue. Its acknowledgement is complete. Time, place, and circumstance, the facts of the case, are the ground of the poem's action: from these issues the idiom, certified speech. It is sometimes argued that Yeats's rhetoric is the imperious kind, that his swans are never swans but symbols conniving with a tangible form. There are a few poems in which the case might be urged. But in the great middle poems the images are palpable to a degree that hardly applies in another modern poet: the houses are houses, the people are people, and if a certain emblematic resonance accrues to them in the poems it is precisely because they are deemed significant and that significance is historical. Yeats lived in an eventful time: when he sought images of value and force he found them there, in events, in time. His phoenix is a historical woman and remains so even when she is identified with Helen of Troy; she never loses her authenticity.

Yeats's spokesman in "Ego Dominus Tuus" justifies his tracing characters upon the sands instead of imitating the great masters: "Because I seek an image, not a book." Thought is not enough, though the poet will sometimes fancy otherwise in *The Tower.* The image he seeks is described by Robartes in "The Phases of the Moon": at the fourteenth phase "the soul begins to tremble into stillness, to die into the labyrinth of itself":

> All thought becomes an image and the soul
> Becomes a body.

The body and the image, I assume, are the dancer and the dance, dynamic, indistinguishable, the final gesture in the dialogue of self and anti-self.

My argument. . .is that in *The Wild Swans at Coole* the balloon of speculation is brought into the shed of common experience: in this book more radically than elsewhere Yeats takes "the living world for text" [*CP,* 131]. We have to realize this before we can register the impassioned gravity of its later pages.

Perhaps this explains why the poems in *The Wild Swans at Coole* seem peculiarly "central" to our experience. The burden of meaning has been placed firmly where it belongs, in people, and in the acts that embody their values. The book is an anthology of represented lives in which private vision becomes incarnate in public action; Lionel Johnson, John Synge, George Pollexfen, Robert Gregory, Solomon and Sheba, Iseult Gonne, the anonymous and the classic fishermen—and many more. The poems speak to us directly, to our sense of the human predicament; and in the last reckoning this is a more reliable mode of communication than the Great Memory or even the Body. The human image in this book is at once sweet and serviceable; it hides behind no platitudes that it can see; it does not feel called upon to take possession of the world or to set up as God. It acknowledges human limitation and tries to live as well as possible under that shadow. The image chimes with our own sense of the "creatural" situation; it is continuous with our own unspectacular experience in its assent to common occasion. . . .

* * *

We must tackle those poems, two especially, which would seem to undermine my general argument about Yeats. . . .The vast majority of his poems from "Adam's Curse" to the very last pages of the great book choose the living world for text; they are poems of place, time, memory, voice, conflict, personality. I do not find there a single poem in which Yeats releases himself from these obligations: he never composed a Supreme Fiction. That he occasionally wished to do so, I would not deny: the poems that spring to mind at once are, of course, the two Byzantine poems.

I have argued on another occasion that the best way to read Yeats's *Collected Poems* is to think of it as dramatizing a great dispute between Self and Soul; Self being all those motives which tie one to earth and time, Soul being the freedom of imagination transcending the finite. The dispute was never resolved. Yeats would lend himself to one side or the other, but always with misgivings, knowing the cost of severance.[10] This is my chief quarrel with those who would read the Byzantine poems as if they were written by Wallace Stevens: these poems are not parables about

[10] In his essay in *An Honoured Guest* (the other "occasion" to which he refers), Donoghue notes that while in certain prose passages "Yeats was prepared to concede, of Self and Soul, that one is as much a part of truth as the other, . . . in most of the poems he enlisted under one banner and—for the time being—served it zealously. In *The Winding Stair,* when it came to a choice between the circuit which carried him into man and that which carried him into God, he chose man; but even as he voted he felt the burden of misgiving, loss, sacrifice, waste." Later in this same essay, Donoghue specifies a related "cost of severance." A Yeatsian poem "aspires to the condition of drama, incorrigibly in time, and it capitalises upon the ambiguities of such terms as role, action, gesture, mask, and play. This is at once the strength and the limitation of the doctrine; when it is utterly dedicated to reality and justice, it is powerful, self-possessed, and humane, always aware of the crime of death and birth. To assume a role and accept the discipline of living it is splendid; but the temptation is merely to flaunt a pose, to strike a gesture, to cut a dash" (*An Honoured Guest,* pp. 115, 120).

the free imagination; they are poems about the dispute of Self and Soul at a time when old age and approaching death seem to vote resoundingly for Soul.

"Sailing to Byzantium" begins with the old man leaving the world and human life, looking back at the sensuality of the shade; partly in wonder, partly in pathos, partly in self-pity. In the second stanza the Self is separated from Soul, as Dublin—shall we say—is separated from the "holy city of Byzantium." The third stanza is a prayer to the new household gods to destroy the antinomies of day and night, resolving everything now in "the artifice of eternity." (Yeats still knows the limitations of this device; if it is eternity it is also artifice.) The last stanza is a furious promise, as if in atonement for all the selfish motives of a temporal life:

> Once out of nature I shall never take
> My bodily form from any natural thing,
> But such a form as Grecian goldsmiths make
> Of hammered gold and gold enamelling
> To keep a drowsy Emperor awake;
> Or set upon a golden bough to sing
> To lords and ladies of Byzantium
> Of what is past, or passing, or to come.

I wonder if it has been noted what a curious song the bird is to sing; almost as strange as the motto given to us by the figures on Keats's Grecian urn. We are out of nature, in Byzantium, in eternity, and yet the burden of the song is "what is past, or passing, or to come"; Self-topics, with a vengeance. Kenneth Burke takes these lines to mean "that 'nature' becomes tyrannously burdensome, once the poet, having made himself at home in 'grace,' finds that it has been withdrawn."[11] Nature is his term, I think, for Self, and Grace for Soul. I read the passage differently, on the principle that Yeats never made himself at home in Soul and dragged the Self with him even into Byzantium. The last lines seem to be a turning-back to the world of time, joining up again, incipiently, with the sensual music of the first stanza.

In the later poem, "Byzantium," a poet, half in sickness, thinks of death. But since death is by definition beyond experience he cannot do much with it, so he finds relief and some dignity in an engaging fancy, the neo-Platonic décor of death. And because he is at least an amateur dramatist he wants to give his images the thrust of action and event; hence his recourse to Dante and the guides. For the time being, the chosen affiliations are identified

[11] Kenneth Burke, *A Rhetoric of Motives* (New York, Braziller, 1955), p. 317. [Donoghue's note]

with Value, and an attempt is made to disengage these from the "fury and the mire of human veins." The poet's choices are temperamental and suitably "aesthetic," but once entertained they keep the needs of the occasion at bay and work up an impressive energy. Because they have an imposing lineage they are self-perpetuating, and Yeats goes along with them. The feelings engaged call for the High Style, not because they carry the freight of doctrine but because the occasion is featuring a ceremonial event, a large showing. Officially, Yeats is opting for the moonlit dome, and he tries to work up a corresponding severity, if not "disdain," for "all that man is." The second stanza begins,

> Before me floats an image, man or shade,
> Shade more than man, more image than a shade;

thus giving us the terms of an ascending sequence, spiralling toward Byzantium. Later in the poem we will be given another set of terms, distinguished in precisely the same way: for man, shade, and image we are now to read bird, handiwork, and miracle:

> Miracle, bird or golden handiwork,
> More miracle than bird or handiwork,

and in any event we are directed thus beyond the natural condition. But this needs a certain pressure, and the second stanza includes one dangerously vatic moment which the style can barely hold: "I hail the superhuman; I call it death-in-life and life-in-death." But the meditative trance continues with a second version of moonlit disdain. In the third stanza the flames on the Emperor's floor are distinguished from their counterparts in the natural world, which otherwise they would dangerously resemble; similarly the dance and the "agony of trance." And then, thinking of the dolphins that carry the human souls to the next world, Yeats "makes the mistake" of adverting to their "mire and blood." Now immediately the dispute of Self and Soul, which seemed to have been resolved by transcendence, breaks out all over again. As I read the poem, this is the saving stanza, as the poet turns his gaze back and out to the sea of human life and the pity of the whole thing rushes into the rhythm, "That dolphin-torn, that going-tormented sea." For me this act certifies the drama, and without it I would assent to the play only sluggishly, for most of it is indeed a performance, however impressive. This mode of poetry is not the highest, because it can hardly have the sublimity of prophecy and anything less, on such an occasion, is bound to be a little fanciful. "Byzantium" is a more spectacular poem than "Sailing to Byzantium," but it is not as fine, as coherent or as just. This is not because the later poem is more dependent upon its handsome symbols but because it commits itself to its presumptive form at a stage somewhat short of moral understanding. It is as if "Byzantium" were a very late draft for a poem never quite completed. Yeats is saying rather less than he seems to claim, making spectacular play with the heuristic possibilities of the symbols. The poem, in short, is weak in moral syntax. Perhaps this explains our hesitation, if we hesitate. The play is spectacular but heady, somewhat hysterical. A chosen tradition plays an important part in the poem, supplying most of the symbols and most of the feeling, but the function of the traditional lore is largely honorific and picturesque; most of it is present to make up a distinguished gathering. The tradition does not test, because there is not enough to test, not enough to criticize, not enough Fact to put to the measure of Value. The domes, bobbins, cocks, and dances reverberate imperiously, and Yeats draws wonderful music from these traditional instruments, but the tradition does not finally grapple with the individual talent. This is why "Sailing to Byzantium" and—to choose another—"Vacillation" seem to me better poems, poems of reality and justice. . . .

* * *

In the winter of 1913–14 Ezra Pound provided secretarial and advisory services for Yeats at Stone Cottage, Coleman's Hatch, "in Sussex by the waste moor." Pound's version is given in Canto 83. . . . The issue between them, it soon becomes clear, is the status of the object, the given world. At the end of *A Vision* Yeats speaks of finding everything in the symbol. In "Sailing to Byzantium" he asks to be gathered into "the artifice of eternity." In Canto 83 the secretary answers, "Le Paradis n'est pas artificiel." This is, to begin, an answer to Baudelaire: one of Baudelaire's books is called *Les Paradis artificiels,* an elaborate chorale to hieroglyphic dreams and symbols.

Canto 83 rebukes Baudelaire and the entire Symbolist tradition as well as Yeats; tactfully, because the critical point has already been made in Cantos 74, 76, and 77. Paradise, Pound implies, is not *artificiel,* an assertion of Symbolist will: it exists, finite and historical, if "only in fragments," like excellent sausage, the smell of mint, and Ladro the night cat. So he makes fun of Yeats:

and Uncle William dawdling around Notre Dame
in search of whatever
paused to admire the symbol
with Notre Dame standing inside it.

I read this as a reflection not upon the church but upon Yeats's sense of it, his tendency to replace the given world by a figment of the Symbolist imagination. Pound is warning Yeats that the given world, such as it is, is more durable than all the bronzes of Symbolism: it stands forth, bodied against the hieroglyphic dream and the golden bird. This criticism of Yeats has often been repeated, but it is wide of the mark. Yeats is not Baudelaire. Indeed, in the context of modern literature his commitment to the finite world as a structure in its own right is remarkable. To relate him to Berkeley and Blake and Nietzsche, without admitting this qualification, is wrong.[12] Sturge Moore saw that in "Sailing to Byzantium" the goldsmith's bird is "as much nature as a man's body," and that it sings of natural things. True, Yeats wrote "Byzantium" partly to answer Moore, but even there the spirit, as we have seen, cannot finally disdain the gong-tormented sea.

This is to say that Yeats was not a Symbolist. We have already argued for this reading. It is also to say that the Gnostic contempt for the given world and the Symbolist resentment of its claims tend to coalesce; and, coalescing, to sponsor that severance of the private and the public worlds which we have mentioned. We come back to the inescapable question: wise and criminal as we are, how to live in this "old chaos of the sun."[13]

[12] Nietzsche, whose commitment was emphatically to the earth, seems out of place here. In fact, in a later volume—*William Butler Yeats,* Viking Press, New York, 1971—Donoghue notes the paramount importance of the Nietzschean influence on Yeats.

[13] Wallace Stevens's phrase, from "Sunday Morning."

Northrop Frye

The Top of the Tower: A Study of the Imagery of Yeats

All poets speak the same symbolic language, but they have to learn it either by instinct or unconsciously from other poets. In the poetry of the Western world from medieval times to our own, there has been a framework for poetic symbolism with four main levels. On the top level is what I should call the Logos vision, which includes the conventional heaven of religion, the place of the presence of God. The central symbol of the Logos vision is the city, the Biblical New Jerusalem, but it is also often described in metaphors taken from mathematics or from music, the two areas being connected by the conception of "harmony." Central to Logos imagery, in all poetry before Newton's time at least, is the image of the orderly stars, moving in spheres which also give out a harmonious music, the archetype of the music we hear. The Logos vision is that of an order of existence designed by an intelligent Creator, and among its musical and mathematical images is that of the dance, which appears in Dante, in Sir John Davies' *Orchestra,* in the Eliot Quartets, and at the end of "Among School Children." In the last poem the image of the chestnut tree, immediately preceding, recalls the traditional image of the earthly paradise, just below the circling stars, in which man was originally placed.

The stars in their courses are all that is now left of the order of nature as God originally designed it: the earthly paradise he established for man was lost with the fall of Adam. But everything

From The Stubborn Structure *by Northrop Frye (Cornell University Press, Ithaca, N.Y., 1970). Copyright © 1970 by Northrop Frye. First published in* The Southern Review, *Summer 1969, pp. 850–871. Reprinted by permission of Northrop Frye.*

that inspires and ennobles man helps him to ascend from the world of his fallen nature to something nearer his original home, traditionally the Earthly Paradise or the Garden of Eden. This ascent of the soul is another area of poetic symbolism that I shall call the Eros vision, because some form of human love almost invariably prompts it. Eros symbolism usually begins with the figure of the alienated poet, who is forced into writing poetry by being frustrated as a lover. The creative life thus appears as what students of animal behavior call a displaced activity, a substituted outlet of a mainly erotic energy. In medieval times this led to the convention begun by the Provençal love poets and expanded by Dante and Petrarch. According to the more typical forms of this, an erotic relation is established between a poet and a lady which does not aim either at marriage or at any sexual "affair," but is intended from the beginning to pass through frustration to sublimation. The lady is too high in virtue or social rank to be sexually attainable: the poet is merely her servant and a servant of the God of Love, who has commanded him to love the lady. The lady then becomes the inspiration for everything good that the poet does, so that his dedication to her may also be an ascent of his soul toward virtue. In the chivalric romances this virtue is symbolized by the courage and strength of the knight-errant as he continues to rid the world of dragons and giants and tyrants. Such a convention is based on an erotic analogy to Christianity, and it was easy to fit it into the medieval Christian framework. In Christianity man has fallen from a higher state of being, and hence a love-inspired ascent of the soul may be thought of as a partial return to its original state, the state symbolized by Adam in Eden. I say a partial return, because for Christianity no one can complete the process in this life: for Catholic Christianity it is completed after death in purgatory.

There are two main varieties of Eros vision, the explicitly sexual and the sublimated. We may call them, following Milton, the allegro and the penseroso visions, though of course they are far older than Milton: Ovid, for example, writes an art of love which moves toward sexual intercourse, and then deals with the "remedies" of love which take the opposite road. Milton's allegro vision is one of "unreprovèd pleasures free" which take the narrator to an earthly Paradise, where Orpheus may hear an erotic (Lydian) music that might restore his Eurydice to him; the penseroso vision is a sublimated love for a nun (vestal virgin) which makes the narrator a philosopher studying Plato in a lonely tower, and leaves him a prophet and hermit. A similar duality in the Eros vision exists in medieval poetry. In *The Romaunt of the Rose* the poet is a lover whose quest ends with his physical possession of his mistress's body: in Dante's *Purgatorio* the poet is impelled by his love for Beatrice to climb the mountain of Purgatory to the Garden of Eden on top of it. There is no sexual culmination: Dante first meets a young girl, Matilda, but he is separated from her by a river; then he meets Beatrice, but Beatrice does not go farther than unveiling her mouth, the visible sex organ, so to speak.

The world that men entered with the fall of Adam and is now born into is a tragic world, and its central image is that of the dying god Adonis or Dionysus, a role which Christ adopts in his Incarnation. The tragic hero often recapitulates the dying god's typical life from mysterious birth to premature death; we also have an episodic form of this theme in the poems that deal with birth in this world as a loss of innocence or fall from a paradisal world to a lower one. Examples include poems by Vaughan and Traherne, Wordsworth's "Intimations of Immortality Ode," Blake's *Book of Thel,* Dylan Thomas's "Fern Hill," and a passage in Yeats's "Among School Children." Below this world of tragic or ironic experience is the Thanatos vision, including the hell of Christianity and the ironic visions of our day which present experience as an unending life in death.

All four of these worlds are clearly marked in Yeats's symbolism. The Logos vision, the "Thirteenth Cone" where Chance and Choice are one, is not often referred to, but it is integral to his imagery none the less. It is most explicitly described, perhaps, in the fourth of the "Supernatural Songs":

> There all the barrel-hoops are knit,
> There all the serpent-tails are bit,
> There all the gyres converge in one,
> There all the planets drop in the Sun.

This world is regularly associated with the sun in Yeats, and it stands above the cycle of life and death represented by the ouroboros or tail-biting serpent of the second line. Yeats tell us that this world in Plato is a world of pure Idea or Form, but that Plotinus transformed it into a "timeless individuality or daimon," preferring Socrates to his thought, and seeing the Logos world existentially as a total person rather than a total idea, containing "archetypes of all possible existences whether of man or brute." Plotinus was, Yeats says, the first to establish this individuality as the sole source of being, though Yeats's Christian and Jewish readers, at least, might feel that a few other people had got to the conception a little earlier than Plotinus. The traditional associations of harmony appear in a remarkable early evocation of this Logos world in the poem "Paudeen":

> on the lonely height where all are in God's eye,
> There cannot be, confusion of our sound forgot,
> A single soul that lacks a sweet crystalline cry.

It is, however, the imagery of Eros that I want to consider more particularly in this essay. The theme of the sexually inspired ascent of the soul underlies the "tower" and "winding stair" images in Yeats. The most obvious source for the images is, again, the spiral *escalina* or staircase going up and around the mountain of Purgatory in Dante. It is interesting that the only other poet producing work of comparable value to that of Yeats, T. S. Eliot, was also fascinated by staircases, and his *Ash Wednesday,* with its winding stair and its explicit debt to the *Purgatorio,* is roughly contemporary with the appearance of the same imagery in Yeats. The spiral shape of Dante's mountain links the winding stair with Yeats's gyre image. The gyre for Yeats is one of the central images of the cycle of life because it can be an emblem either of fertility and life or of death. The former produces the cornucopia or horn of plenty, an image appearing in "A Prayer for My Daughter," and the latter the Charybdis or maelstrom. The activity of the poet, moving from a broad receptivity to the concentrated effort of creation, may be thought of as a spiral or vortex of energy moving from base to apex. This activity recapitulates, in its turn, the whole movement of life, of plants from receptive root to climactic fruit or blossom, and of animals, who pass through the vortex of birth from one world to another. Once entered into the world of birth, another vortex pulls them back through its apex into death, which is symbolically a return to the mother. The death-gyre appears in Dante's hell, which, like his purgatory, is a cone narrowing from base to apex.

The gyre is of course also a sexual symbol, male on the outside and female on the inside, and sex is closely connected with rising flames and the spiralling of smoke, fire being a traditional purgatorial image also. We may compare the rites of kindling the "need-fire" described in *The Golden Bough,* where a naked boy and girl go into a room together and make fire by twirling a pointed stick in a hole, or what Yeats calls perning in a gyre. Sexual intercourse and the birth resulting from it form a double gyre or reversing movement into and out of the mother's body. The seashell, which appears in the first poem in Yeats's *Collected Poems,* is another helical emblem of life arising out of the sea, and the ear, described by Blake, in a more sinister context, as "a whirlpool fierce to draw creations in," is the vortex through which the Word is born in the Virgin's body in Yeats's "Mother of God." Dante's greatest predecessor as an Eros poet was Plato, whose ascent of the soul is usually associated with the ladder. But, if we can believe Aristophanes' *The Clouds,* where Socrates is represented as dethroning the gods and replacing them with a new deity called *dinos* or "whirl," perhaps the gyre underlies the Socratic tradition too.

In the Bible the ascent from earth to heaven is also first represented by a ladder, the image of Jacob's, that is, Israel's, dream. From the point of view of later Christian typology, this ladder would be identical spiritually with the later journey of Israel as a people through the labyrinth of the desert toward their original home or Promised Land. The gyre is a conventionalized labyrinth, the crooked path of the serpent as distinct from the straight path of the arrow. The Promised Land is symbolically identical with the original Garden of Eden, and is represented in the New Testament by the vision of the Virgin Mother and her divine Child, the epiphany of divine innocence. The connecting link between the Promised Land and the Virgin is the *hortus conclusus* or enclosed garden of the Song of Songs, identified with the body of the Virgin in Christian symbolism. All these Biblical archetypes are incorporated in Dante. Dante begins with the standard medieval Eros theme, the alienated lover who is inspired by his love in the form of a vision. He goes up the Mountain of Purgatory, shedding one of the seven deadly sins at each stage, the last sin to be purged being, appropriately enough, lechery or excessive physical love, where again the image of fire appears. After this Dante finds himself in Eden, so that he has really regained his own childhood, not his individual childhood but his generic childhood as a son of Adam.

Thus Dante's quest up the Mountain has in a sense gone backward in time, removing the sins which accumulated in his ordinary experience like, to use a Yeatsian image, the wrappings of a mummy cloth around a mummy, and thus proceeding from his situation as a poet in mid-career back to the ultimate source of his life. Similarly, Yeats says of the spirits in his equivalent of purgatory: "They examine their past if undisturbed by our importunity, tracing events to their source, and as they take the form their thought suggests, seem to live backward through time." After Virgil has left Dante with a grave benediction, in possession of his free will, his own pope and emperor, Beatrice appears, scolding like an Italian mamma, and Dante is immediately reduced to a whimpering and tearful child. An erotic impulse drives Dante from the sexual into the pre-sexual, and from there to his own original state of innocence. It looks as though, psychologically, one of the goals of the Eros ascent is connected with the mother and the mother's encircling body (one thinks of another modern treatment of the theme in Auden's and Isherwood's *Ascent of F6*).

As the lover or visionary proceeds on his quest toward his own eternal youth, the shadow of ordinary life appears beside him in the form of an old man, who guides and instructs him on the journey but cannot enter the final paradise. This figure is represented by Moses in the Exodus story and by Virgil in Dante. In the New Testament we have Joseph, who also cannot enter the *hortus conclusus,* as well as the Magi of Matthew and the Simeon of Luke. I have mentioned Milton's allegro and penseroso visions, where there is a modulation of this theme. The figure of the philosopher in the tower, studying the stars of the Logos vision, is linked by Yeats both with Il Penseroso and with Shelley's Prince Athanase. In Milton's *Comus* the usual associations of hero or heroine and guardian are reversed: the Lady's chastity puts her in tune with the Logos harmonies of the heavenly world, but her attendant spirit goes back to an earthly Paradise, identified with Spenser's Gardens of Adonis, of which more later. Most comedy is written in the Eros mode, and we notice in Shakespeare the penseroso figures of Jaques and Prospero, who withdraw from the festivity and multiple marriages at the end into a meditative solitude.

In Yeats the theme of a journey backward in time is reinforced by the "ancestral stair" in which the poet travels in the track of his great predecessors, and by the personal and cultural memories in "The Tower." Long before Yeats had made what he calls "the connection, still vague in my imagination, between pilgrimage and vision, scenery and the pilgrim's salvation," he had picked up the conception of two levels of existence, one that of ordinary life and the other a land of eternal youth, from the Irish legends of the Tir na nOg and the Sidhe dancing in the gyres of the whirling wind. In many stories of fairyland, the mortals who enter it find that time is arrested there, and that when they return to ordinary life they have become incredibly aged, in the role of the old man cast out of the earthly paradise.[1]

There has been, as already indicated, an old feud between the sexual and the sublimated or religious versions of the Eros quest, and even in the sublimated versions some ambiguity recurs. The Israelites were able to enter the Promised Land only through the help of the harlot Rahab, and Rahab in Dante marks the boundary of what is in effect the total area of the lower Paradise, which

[1] This is the hero's fate in Yeats's narrative poem *The Wanderings of Oisin.*

stretches from the Garden of Eden, at the top of Mount Purgatory, just below the moon, to the sphere of Venus, the limit of the earth's shadow in Dante's astronomy. Rahab, the last soul seen in Venus, balances the figure of Matilda, the first soul seen in Eden. Similarly, the story of the Virgin Birth in the Bible comes very close to being a story of a forgiven harlot, and the forgiven harlot appears in the Gospels and later legends in the form of another Mary. In most paintings of the Crucifixion, Christ is flanked by both Marys, the forgiven harlot in red and the Virgin in blue. There is a similar duality in Yeats's portrayals of two aspects of the personality, one seeking the sexual cycle and the other trying to escape from it: an early example presents it in its true colors:

> She opened her door and her window,
> And the heart and the soul came through,
> To her right hand came the red one,
> To her left hand came the blue. ["The Cap and Bells," *CP*, 62]

For a complete Eros vision, therefore, we need a virgin, a child, and a harlot. When we add to them the eagle which flies upward into the Logos unity of the sun, and the lion which wanders alone in the wilderness, we have the five elements "That make the Muses sing" ["Those Images," *CP*, 316].

In Dante, the Mountain of Purgatory stands on an island on the other side of the earth, and the souls of the dead reach it by crossing water on the ship of death. As Dante emerges from hell, an angel arrives with a boatload of souls, dumps them down at the foot of the mountain, and hurries back for more. Similarly the wandering of Israel in the desert begins with the crossing of the Red Sea (identical with the escape from Egypt, which is symbolically under the Red Sea with Pharaoh's army). The ancient ship of death image enters Yeat's poem "His Dream," in *The Green Helmet* volume, but in "Byzantium" and in "News for the Delphic Oracle" the vehicular form, as Blake would call it, is not a ship but a dolphin, an equally traditional image of salvation out of the sea. The ascent up the desert mountain culminates in the vision of unfallen nature, symbolized as a rule by an unspoiled or redeemed female. Sometimes this female figure is identified with the moon, the traditional boundary between temporal and eternal worlds, which stands directly above the mountain in Dante and elsewhere. Thus the quest for ideal beauty of Keats's hero Endymion is represented by Endymion's love for Phoebe the moon goddess. In Spenser's Mutabilitie Cantos a great debate, anticipating some of the similar debates in Yeats, is held in the sphere of the moon, which is also just above the top of an Irish mountain, "Arlo Hill." The debate is between Mutability, the ruler of everything below the moon, who claims that everything above the moon is also hers, and Jove, the representative of the higher order of nature. The judge is Nature herself, who decides in favor of Jove, though she admits that there are cycles, and therefore some principle of change, on both levels. In other words, it is essential for a Renaissance Christian poet to keep a higher Logos vision above an Eros one.

The sublimated version of the Eros quest has been more popular in the past, not only for religious reasons, but because of the underlying paradox in the sexual relation expressed by Sir Thomas Browne: "United souls are not satisfied with embraces, but desire to be truly each other." Poets insist on the imagery of mutual identity anyway, though, as we see in Donne's "The Extasie" and Shakespeare's "The Phoenix and the Turtle," usually with some underlying humor and sense of the paradox involved. This tone of paradoxical humor recurs in Yeats's "Solomon and the Witch," where it is suggested that perfect sexual intercourse would restore the fallen world to its paradisal form. But perfect intercourse would be, as Blake says, a complete union of bodies rather than "a pompous high priest entering by a secret place." The capacity for such complete union is ascribed to the angels by Swedenborg, in a passage frequently referred to by Yeats, and one which connects this theme with that of a world adjacent to but different from ours where time runs backward from age towards youth.

In the course of history there are certain gigantic cycles which are started off by a supernatural sex act of this kind, of the type preserved in mythology by the legends of the intercourse of a male bird and a woman, Leda and the swan, the Dove and the Virgin, Attracta and the Irish heron. Such cycles are marked by certain "conjunctions"—an astrological term with an obvious sexual overtone—of planets. The word "consummation" also has a sexual meaning, though in Christian theology it refers primarily to the eventual burning up of the world by fire. But fire, we saw, is a sexual image too, appearing in Dante's ring of fire and Shakespeare's phoenix, and Blake says in *The Marriage of Heaven and Hell* that the apocalypse by fire will take place through "an improvement of sensual enjoyment." This image of the flame of the apocalypse being lit by sex comes into the image at the end of ["In Memory of Eva Gore-Booth and Con Markiewicz"] where the poet strikes a match to set fire to "the great gazebo," which is now a structure of guilt.

Yeats carries his preference for the sexual to the sublimated quest to the point of making several parodies of the latter. The early volume *Responsibilities* is polarized in its symbolism between the figures of the sleeper and the wanderer, the figure who, like the traditional Enoch and Elijah, remains quietly awaiting the final end of things, and the figure who, like Cain or the Wandering Jew, is condemned to wander in the cycle of time. The latter figure is closely connected with the old man who is prevented from entering the earthly paradise, and appears in *Last Poems* as the "pilgrim" and the "wild old wicked man," who gets randier as he gets older. Then again, we saw that in traditional Christian symbolism the higher Logos vision is described in mathematical imagery, which indicates the Christian sense of the superiority of the sublimated and conceptual vision over the sexual one. Yeats makes the point that the element of mathematical formality in Greek art does not transcend the sexual but is itself a powerful expression of the sexual. The art that "Pythagoras planned" turns out to be an apotheosis of physical and sexual beauty, and the same is true of Renaissance art:

> Michael Angelo left a proof
> On the Sistine Chapel roof,
> Where but half-awakened Adam
> Can disturb globe-trotting Madam
> Till her bowels are in heat.

On the other hand, Ribh denounces Patrick for being obsessed by a mathematical notion of a divine Trinity and replacing the old sexual trinity of father, mother, and child with it. Plotinus, whose vision culminates in a flight of the solitary to the solitary, and who was said by his biographer to have been ashamed of being in the body, makes some surprising discoveries about his spiritual goal when he finally reaches it.[2]

In *The Shadowy Waters* the hero and heroine are led on by Aengus, the Irish Eros, towards a world of total love in which the frustrations of ordinary experience have ceased to exist. Consequently they are leaving the world for a paradise:

> . . . in some island where the life of the world
> Leaps upward, as if all the streams o' the world
> Had run into one fountain. [*VP,* 249]

We recall that in the Song of Songs the image of the enclosed garden is paired with that of a "fountain sealed," and the Eros

[2] For the poems alluded to or quoted in this paragraph, see *CP,* 114, 119, 310, 307, 322, 341, 323, 283.

image of journeying upstream to the source or spring of a river appears later in "The Tower" and elsewhere. *The Shadowy Waters* quest reaches a point at the limit of the cyclical world of time, where it impinges on the eternal world. The cycle of time is often symbolized in literature by a dragon or serpent, particularly the ouroboros serpent with its tail in its mouth, referred to in the "Supernatural Song" quoted above. Whether or not the ouroboros is the precise image in Yeats's mind in *The Shadowy Waters,* at any rate Dectora says:

> O ancient worm,
> Dragon that loved the world and held us to it,
> You are broken, you are broken. [*CPl,* 109]

The sailors, on the other hand, follow the cycle and return to the world of time, laden with the treasure that is the more conventional reward of killing the dragon. In *The Herne's Egg,* although there is the apocalyptic embrace of the heron with his priestess, the priestess also requires a sexual act with a human lover in the cycle of time, in order to provide a womb for the body of the dead [Congal] seeking reincarnation, a theme which Yeats adapts from a sardonic Tibetan folk tale.

These examples suggest that there are in fact three possible conclusions for the Eros ascent: the sublimated, the sexual, and the return back down the mountain to ordinary existence. In Dante it is impossible to go back down: the sacramental cable car runs in only one direction. But that is because ordinary life, running from birth to death, has already taken place: purgatory is the reversing movement after death, and for the same reason only the sublimated goal is possible for Dante. Obviously the sexual goal and the return are closely connected, for the natural result of intercourse with the bride is birth, and birth begins the descending movement. One reason why Virgil in Dante cannot get past the top of purgatory is that his imagination reached its limit, from Dante's point of view, in his vision of a world renewed by the birth of a divine child in the Fourth Eclogue. Renewal in time merely turns the cycle of time.

Yet even in Dante there is a faint suggestion that from Eden on top of the mountain all forms of life except human ones fall back into the lower world, and in Spenser's description of the Gardens of Adonis, or sexual earthly paradise, there is a "Time," who is continually forcing seeds and embryos out of this world into the lower one. We saw that the typical figure of the descending movement from birth to death is Adonis, who forsakes the love of

Venus for war and hunting, and who is killed when still young. Adonis symbolism thus complements Eros symbolism. In Christianity the downward journey is preeminently the journey of Christ from Incarnation to Crucifixion, the Agape or descent of love from creator to creature, in which Christ takes on an Adonis or dying-god role, clothed in Luvah's robes of blood, as Blake says, Luvah or Orc being Blake's Eros-Adonis figure. This journey is made by Christ in his capacity as the second Adam, a conscious and voluntary descent repeating and redeeming the first Adam's passionate fall. Thus Spenser, after writing two Hymns on Love and Beauty in the regular Eros convention, follows them with a "Hymn of Heavenly Love" describing the incarnation of Christ. The response of Christian faith to Christ's act forms one of the sublimated versions of the Eros ascent, the version symbolized by Eliot in "Little Gidding" as the ascending movement of fire. The conception of the Eros journey as a reversal of or response to a previous fall is Platonic also, though it is the Neoplatonists rather than Plato who lay stress on the original fall of the soul. Neoplatonic imagery merges with Christianity in the poems about the fall from innocence in childhood already mentioned.

Yeats was, as his *Autobiographies* tell us, fascinated by the notion of a double movement in life, and in the early play *The Hour-Glass* the conception of an antithetical world, whose summer is our winter, is presented in the symbol of the hour-glass itself, the image of time as a double gyre, narrowing and broadening simultaneously. Thus the goal of the Eros ascent, the "land of heart's desire," was from the beginning linked to the tragedy and irony of the world of experience. The goal of the journey of love is usually beauty in some form or other, often an ideal beauty which combines the allegro figure of the imprisoned or sleeping maiden with the penseroso sense of harmony and order. A medieval symbol for such a goal of vision is the Holy Grail, which has female associations in its chalice shape and in its functions as a provider of food and as the container of the body or blood of Christ. The corresponding symbol in Yeats's early poetry is the rose, the symbol of sexual passion as the lily is of virginity, a symbol, as Yeats says, corresponding also to Shelley's intellectual beauty, except that he sees it "as suffering with man and not as something pursued and seen from afar." The phrase implies, among other things, the interconnection of Eros and Adonis symbols. The rose is on the rood of time, just as, in "The Two Trees," the tree of life is reflected in the tree of death. The colors of Eros are the red and white of St. Valentine, the patron of coupling birds like Shakespeare's red phoenix and white turtle; the colors of Adonis are the white and red of the dead body and spilled blood. These colors recur in an episode of the Parzival legend referred to by Yeats, where Parzival sees some blood drops on snow reminding him of his mistress so vividly that he falls into a trance. The poet-lover, inspired by Eros, moves upward toward a female figure who may be virgin mother or mistress; the hero, the incarnation of Adonis, is frequently born of a calumniated mother who may also be a virgin or mistress of a divine bird. Eros shoots arrows, and Adonis figures like St. Sebastian are stuck full of them; Eros seeks his mother Venus, and Adonis escapes Venus to go to his death. In some versions of the dying-god story, including the one Yeats prefers, Adonis is killed by Venus, or rather by the figure whom Robert Graves calls the white goddess, Blake Tirzah or the sinister mother, and Yeats the "staring virgin" [*CP,* 210]. The complementary nature of Eros and Adonis imagery comes out vividly in "Parnell's Funeral":

> A beautiful seated boy; a sacred bow;
> A woman, and an arrow on a string;
> A pierced boy, image of a star laid low.
> That woman, the Great Mother imaging,
> Cut out his heart.

The torn-out heart and the severed head are the two most frequent images of the martyrdom of the hero: they have also some connection with the four suits of cards featured in the Hanrahan stories. Lance and chalice (the two red suits) are the emblems of the Passion of Christ; sword and dish symbolize the death of John the Baptist, who was born at the summer solstice, as Christ was at the winter solstice, decreasing as Christ increases in a double gyre relation to him. Except for one very significant passage in *A Vision* (p. 212), there is not much about John the Baptist in Yeats, but there is a fair amount about Salome, one of the manifestations of the "staring virgin."

Yeats had grasped, even before Frazer's *Golden Bough* appeared, the identity in symbolism between the dying Christ and the Classical dying gods. The association he made all his life between Christ and Dionysus appears as early as "The Secret Rose," where the rose may be sought either in the Holy Sepulchre or in the wine vat. The Adonis symbols in Yeats cluster around two central and traditional images. One is the image of hunting. The Celtic hounds of the other world, white with red ears, appear in the earlier poems with sexual associations, representing, according to Yeats, the frustrated and elusive pursuits of the sex war. Similar animals reappear in the "Hound Voice" of *Last Poems* and in the silenced dogs of "To Dorothy Wellesley," and the theme of "violence of horses" [*CP,* 207] incorporates the archetype of the Wild Hunt into the anarchy of Yeats's own time. The other is the image of the tangled and bloody wood, associated with the setting sun, where the hero lies dead or hung on a tree like Absalom, gored by a beast like Adonis, or torn to pieces by drunken Bacchantes like Orpheus. This wood forms the setting of "Her Vision in the Wood," a poem in *A Woman Young and Old.*

We said that *The Shadowy Waters* portrays two lovers escaping to a paradisal Eros world, while the sailors return to the ordinary one. There had previously been threats of mutiny and conspiracy from the sailors, hence this poem is the earliest example in Yeats of the theme of debate at or near the limit of the Eros journey, which recurs in "A Dialogue of Self and Soul" and "Vacillation." The point on the boundary of the cycle of this world and an immortal world above it, usually associated with the earthly paradise or the moon, or both, the symbolic top of the tower or mountain, is what I have elsewhere called the point of epiphany. In "A Dialogue of Self and Soul" the soul is a disciple of Plotinus, and wants to go upward from the point of epiphany into the pure mystical identity of solitude of which Plotinus speaks. The self looks downward, fascinated by the Adonis symbols of the ceremonial sword and its silk covering embroidered with flowers of "heart's purple." Those things are "Emblematical of love and war," and the soul wants no part of them. The self speaks for the poet, who, unlike the mystic, is committed to images, to sense experience, and to the recurring wheel of life. It is clear that the Eros dialogue between the wise old guide and the impetuous lover is not always a matter of the guide's informing his charge. Perhaps, however, we should think of both speakers as aspects of the old man in the tower, as a development of the two figures of *Responsibilities* previously mentioned, the sleeper and the wanderer: those who await a final consummation either in repose or in restlessness.

We are left with a strong impression that, as in Eliot, the way up and the way down are the same (except that Eliot's directions are reversed, the "dark night" vision being the upward one in Yeats), and that if one succeeds in either, one gets both. It should be noticed, however, that the soul associates *guilt* with the double gyre of descent and return, speaking of "the *crime* of death and birth," and that the self does not finally accept guilt. In his resolve to "cast out remorse" the self's proposed descent is more like that of the bodhisattva in Eastern religions, and what he reaches by descent is the genuine Earthly Paradise, the total vision of innocence in which, going even beyond Blake's "Everything that lives is holy," he can say "Everything we look upon is blest."

In "Among School Children" there is again a contrast between the nun, whose image retains "a marble or a bronze repose," and the mother, who is bound to the cycle of recurrence. Here the two ideals are seen more ironically as equally half-achievements, perfection being symbolized by the tree and the dancer, in whom spontaneity and discipline, vitality and harmony, have become the same thing, and where the body has not been broken by the soul, like the nun's, or by birth, like the mother's. "Vacillation" begins with one of the standard point-of-epiphany symbols, the tree of life or "labyrinth of the birds," also represented by the chestnut tree in "Among School Children" and the living tree with its demonic reflection in "The Two Trees." In "Vacillation," as in "The Two Trees," the tree has two aspects, one of which is the "Attis" tree on which the dying god, or his image, is hung. This tree thus again illustrates the interconnection of innocence and experience, Eros and Adonis. Here again the poet considers the sublimated goal of the perfection of life, whose symbol, a subtler one than the "marble and bronze" of "Among School Children," is the incorruptible body of the dead saint. The poet again, however, chooses the cycle of death and rebirth out of corruption, the lion and honeycomb of Samson's riddle, though without challenging the traditional moral contrast between corruptible and incorruptible body.

Yeats, then, consistently rejects for himself, though not necessarily for anyone else, the sublimated goals of the Eros vision that lead on to the Logos vision, and prefers the sexual goal which leads inevitably to going back down into the cycle again. Because he is a poet, Yeats tells us, he must choose the path of the hero and the "swordsman" rather than the saint [*L,* 798]. This is not simply a temperamental choice: there is a major complication in Yeats's winding-stair imagery that did not exist for, say, Dante. In Christianity, and in Neoplatonism more speculatively, the sublimation of the sexual instinct is the preferred program, because the man inspired by love is ultimately not seeking a sexual partner, but is a creature returning to his creator. But for Yeats there is no creator in the picture except man himself. The sources of creation are not in a divine mind beyond the stars: they are in the "foul rag-and-bone shop of the heart" at the *bottom* of the ladder. The alienation symbolized by the disdainful mistress of Eros poetry and by the "staring virgin" of Adonis poetry, who tear out the poet's or hero's heart, is the point to which all creation regularly recurs. To return to his creator, man has to come back down again, return on himself, seek the source of the creative powers which are close to the sexual instincts, and are therefore in "the place of excrement," as Crazy Jane says [*CP,* 254], partaking of the corruption out of which all life comes.

What is the consequence of such a choice? One consequence certainly is the incorporation into Yeats's imagery of a purely ironic view of human life and history, in which all things are ordered by a relentlessly turning cycle. The cycle is the form that the double gyre assumes when it becomes the controlling image of all life. It is a central doctrine of *A Vision* that reality can manifest itself only in a series of opposites, a doctrine Yeats associates with Nicholas Cusanus, as Joyce associates it with Bruno, and seeing a double gyre as a single cycle is the same principle in reverse. This cyclical and fatalistic view of history is the one that is set out in *A Vision.* The fatalism of *A Vision* is in part a reflection of the passivity of mind in which Yeats received it, but even so it is important to realize that *A Vision* is Yeats's *Inferno,* his demonic or Thanatos vision. We said that the Eros theme, which enters into the Petrarchan or Courtly Love convention, normally begins with frustration, in which the lover complains of and bewails the inflexible cruelty of his lady. Yeats's love for Maud Gonne provides the corresponding theme in his poetry, and Maud Gonne is repeatedly associated with Helen of Troy. Helen of Troy in turn, hatched from the egg of Leda, is the symbol of the eternal recurrence of history, the misery she caused inevitably repeating itself in future ages. We are not surprised to find *A Vision* astrological in symbolism: all hells contain parodies of heavens, and visions of harmony and fatality alike tend to be astrological in reference.

We are not surprised either to find the imagery of *A Vision* completely dominated by

> the circle of the moon
> That pitches common things about [*CP,* 204],

for, in the traditional cosmology we have been dealing with, the world of the closed cycle of time is a sublunar world. Solar imagery never gets really integrated into *A Vision,* and references to solar symbolism elsewhere in Yeats suggest a pattern of far greater comprehensiveness than *A Vision* ever achieved. The same ironic sublunar perspective comes into "Blood and the Moon," which turns on the melancholy adage *si la jeunesse savait, si la vieillesse pouvait.* The Eros vision of youth is inseparable from the Adonis vision with its premature death and its "odour of blood," and the vision of wisdom pursued by age is an attempt to grasp the static order of something that must be dead before it can be understood. In this perspective every civilization leaves its structure unfinished, dying at the top, like [Burke] and his tree, and the rare individual who gets near the top finds only an empty lumber room full of dead butterflies. In this ironic perspective the "tower" built by human creative power is a structure of pride and arrogance, identical with the Tower of Babel which stretched upwards towards the moon, only to be abandoned to ruin by dissensions in the mob. It is also the great "clock tower" which marks but never escapes from the wheel of time. In the end it becomes the "black tower" of death, where "the dead upright" are watched by an immovable guard.[3] At the end of "Blood and the Moon" the moon appears, symbol, as it so often is, of a teasing and elusive perfection which is out of the reach of both the red blood of power and the white bones of wisdom. The moon stared at by the cat Minnaloushe is the image of a cycle that is always changing and yet never changing, as Oedipus kills his father and Cuchulain his son, age after age, through earth and purgatory alike. Behind it are the greater cycles symbolized by the "Full Moon in March," associated with the two great events of what may have been the one period of decisive change in history, the period between the death of Julius Caesar and the resurrection of Jesus Christ.

In *A Vision,* human life struggles upward to the complete subjectivity of Phase Fifteen and downward to the complete objectivity of Phase One without ever attaining either. The struggle upward is said to be toward nature and the struggle downward toward God, but the completely natural Phase Fifteen is supernatural, and at Phase One "God" occupies the place of death. What is really at Phase One is the mob, the undifferentiated mass of a late civilization, the mob to which "Church and State" have been reduced in Yeats's time, according to the poem of that name, and which every great man, or at least every great Irishman, has despised. The "primary" mob is Yeats's Satan, the accuser of mankind. It accuses by making the standard appeals of slave morality, the appeals to conscience, equality, and altruism. In short, it inspired the guilt ridden political activism of Maud Gonne and the Gore-Booth sisters. The dragon that kills the hero is, ultimately, the mob that drags him down, as the Irish mob slandered Parnell, attacked Synge, and murdered O'Higgins. One thinks of Spenser's Blatant Beast, the emblem of slander and envy. The opinionated female, according to one of Yeats's more tedious themes, ex-

[3] The references are to Yeats's play *The King of the Great Clock Tower* and his poem "The Black Tower" (*CP,* 340).

pressed in "Michael Robartes and the Dancer" and elsewhere, fights for the dragon instead of the knight trying to rescue her, and thereby impersonates the "staring virgin" tearing out the hero's heart.[4] A more serious aspect of this theme is the connection between Christianity and slave morality which made the sacrifice of Christ, according to *Calvary,* an outrage to Judas and Lazarus and meaningless to the heron and the swan, emblems of an "antithetical" cycle which complements and completes the "primary" half-achievement of Christ.

It is important to notice that the great wheel of *A Vision* turns in the opposite direction from the Eros-Adonis cycle. In the latter the comic rises and the tragic falls. All our language about comedy and tragedy, such as the metaphor in "catastrophe," and the word *fall* itself, shows how inevitable these associations are. But in *A Vision* Yeats is interested in the heroic rather than the tragic, and associates comedy with the kind of realism that he regarded as decadent. Hence in *A Vision* the tragic and heroic are the "antithetical" themes that rise out of the mass, and the comic is the "primary" mass that pulls everything down to itself. This introduces into the poetry certain tragic aspects of the Eros ascent, with the proud Furies climbing the stair of the bloody tower in "To Dorothy Wellesley," and with the "odour of blood on the ancestral stair" in "Blood and the Moon." Similarly, there is an innocent aspect of tragedy, which is the inward exuberance or gaiety of the heroic spirit, a gaiety much insisted on in the later poems, notably "Lapis Lazuli." Such gaiety is unaffected by the tragic or ironic aspects of the world it is in, and which are seen only from the outside. It enables heroes like "the great lord of Chou" in "Vacillation" to say "Let all things pass away" in triumph or in disaster alike, the moment of experience having the reality that anything which dissolves in time misses. It is also this gay science, as it has been called, that encourages the poet to identify himself with the process of death and corruption and rebirth instead of attempting to escape from it like the saint or mystic.

We began by saying that traditionally there is a Logos vision in poetry, a vision of an intelligently ordered nature, and that this vision can also be found in Yeats. But the Logos vision is, again, traditionally attained only after an arduous upward striving of the soul, and . . . Yeats, once he has attained this point, deliberately turns his back on the Logos vision and goes downward again. This in turn brings him into an infernal or ironic vision of an unending cyclical alternation of forces all through history. But, we said, the

[4] For the poems alluded to, see *CP,* 229, 181, 333, 108, 109, 230, 187, 210.

real reason for Yeats's turning away from the Logos vision was that for him the sources of creation were within man, in the corruption of the human heart. The language of symbolism usually begins with a creation myth, the story of how things came to be. In the history of mythology, it is the sexual creation myths that come first, stories of how the world was born, or revived like spring from winter. Such myths are centered on an earth-mother, and the more sophisticated myths of a sky-father who *makes* the world and imposes an intelligible pattern on it come later. Yeats speaks of

> the red-rose-bordered hem
> Of her, whose history began
> Before God made the angelic clan. [*CP,* 49]

It is the mother-centered sexual myth that Yeats appears to follow back to its source in the return to the mother which is at once birth and death, womb and tomb.

But having made this descent, Yeats finds that he has once again been sliding down half of a double gyre, this time the one given us by Heraclitus. Once he has made his journey to the heart of the corruptible, he finds that he can now go back again, up from the "fury and mire" of human veins toward a dry light, or genuine Logos vision (Heraclitus also uses the term *Logos*), in which the gleaming city of light is seen once more, but seen this time as a city whose maker and builder is man. The contrast between Yeats and Shelley on this point is instructive. Yeats speaks of Shelley as "constantly" using towers as poetic images, and it is true that the word occurs very frequently in Shelley. But when it means a building, Shelley's tower tends to be a rather sinister image, like the "Tower of Famine" or the madhouse in *Julian and Maddalo.* Towers used apocalyptically, along with "domes" and "pyramids," are often not buildings, but mountains or clouds or other images of a regenerate nature. This is true even of the *Prometheus Unbound* passage misquoted by Yeats in "Blood and the Moon," and even Prince Athanase only sits apart from men "*as* in a lonely tower." Shelley is certainly a poet in the Eros tradition of Plato and Dante, but his contemplative counterpart of the Earthly Paradise (as presented in "The Sensitive Plant" and elsewhere) is rather the oracular cave, a much more obviously maternal symbol. The point is small but significant: Shelley, who died at thirty, revolves around an identification of man and a feminine nature; and Yeats's tower, building, and city imagery indicates a symbolism appropriate to an art that looks beyond nature into "the artifice of eternity." Like Blake, Yeats finds his real hero not in the Orc of the sexual and historical cycle, much less in the old man Urizen with his premature Logos vision, but in Los the blacksmith, the creative power that builds the eternal golden city out of time.

In "Sailing to Byzantium" the city is seen from afar, and the tower has expanded into an entire chain of being, ranging from the divine ("drowsy Emperor") through the spiritual (traditionally the angels and the stars, here the sages in the fire) and the human ("lords and ladies of Byzantium") down through the rest of creation with the bird and the tree transformed into gold. "Sailing to Byzantium" is very like a conventional Christian poem about the New Jerusalem awaiting the soul after death, except for the paradox in "the artifice of eternity." The builder of Byzantium is not a God conceived as independent of man, and when man is thought of as the only visible creator, nature is no longer a creation but a ruin, and man builds his palaces out of and in defiance of nature. In such a world the tree no longer has the "blind lush leaf" of the dying Attis, but is golden only; yet its gold is not the "staring fury" of "Vacillation" either. Just as the imagery both of the traditional Logos vision and of Yeats's ironic *Vision* is astrological, so the image of Byzantium arising out of the sea of death is alchemical, alchemy being the symbol of a creative *process* in which humanity and nature alike are burned up in the "consummation" of an immortal world of gold, the Golden Age come again.

This reversal of perspective from descent to the corrupt source of creation back up again through the process of creation is a reversal which affects the whole personality, not merely the technical skill of the poet. In *The Shadowy Waters* we are told that those who live ordinary passion-driven lives are helpless puppets of a dream dreamed by the gods. Their passions seem to operate on them as external forces, because of course the gods who are dreaming them are their own projected selves. In their view of things, this passive puppet-life is reality, and genuine desire, as expressed in dreams and in love, seems utterly impotent against it. The dreamer, the lover, and the poet are all engaged in reversing the current of reality: they are identifying themselves with the true gods, who are the powers of dream and love and creation themselves. These powers have become reality for them, and what the world calls reality has subsided into dream, the world of "living" that ought to be left to servants.[5] The true gods are the "fire-born moods" of an early poem [*CP,* 54], the "Presences" of

[5] Villiers de l'Isle Adam's line from *Axel*—"as for living—our servants will do that for us"—became a motto for Aesthetes and Decadents; Yeats quoted it several times in his *Autobiography.*

"Among School Children," and the "Daimon" of the later, profounder, and yet less well understood parts of *A Vision.*

In "Byzantium" the imagery is again Heraclitean and alchemical, the vision of "Sailing to Byzantium" seen from within as a process. We start out in the sea, the beginning and the end of life, and move from the "fury and mire" of human passion upward to the "changeless metal." This is the movement of discarnation, opposite to the birth-to-death movement of incarnation, in which the spiral wrappings of the dead mummy are unwound, a movement that takes us beyond the world that is "by the moon embittered," and where the gong never ceases to strike. Perhaps, then, the intuition of so many poets, including Dante, that this journey of the soul is also connected with another life after ordinary death has something to be said for it. If man has invented death, as Yeats says, he can recover what he has projected, and find his home in the "translunar Paradise" which he himself can make, and has made [*CP,* 196, 230].

The poet of the Byzantium poems has gone far beyond the mystery of the Fifteenth Phase of *A Vision,* presented there as something forever beyond human capacities. The Fifteenth Phase is guarded, we are told, by Christ and Buddha. Christ descended into the bottom of the cyclical world—made himself of no account, as Paul says—and then rose out of it, with a great company following. Buddha meditated on the deliverance of man from his own Narcissus image, "mirror on mirror mirrored," the genuine Hercules in heaven liberated from his shadow in Hades.[6] Just as in Eliot's "Burnt Norton" the summit of vision and the depth of annihilation are the same point, the still point of the turning world, so in Yeats the top of the tower is both the rag-and-bone shop of the heart and the translunar Paradise that the heart alone has created.

[6] See *CP,* 167, 322, and the final page of *A Vision.*

M. L. Rosenthal

Visiting Yeats's Tower

Flourish or not, my vocation is to be
the poet of a lifetime, as was he,
and range that lifetime against my fantasy—
my poor knowledge against my threadbare belief.
I too must riddle, "Perfection of the life,
or of the work?"—must find my tower, bring my wife
and children up round the stairway, for all to see
them cower on the battlements with me.

A clown's hubris, to mask the naked face
with a still more naked, vulnerable grimace,
mimic the spiralings of our spinning race
with a sweaty bourgeois climb, and, at tower-top poised,
wheeze through a tickling throat: "Life? Work? My voice
cracks and wobbles, yet Song is my only choice!"
Resonant, impenetrable still, that place
we'd thought to reach, reality's sheer grace.

Reality is here, green, drowsy, around
Yeats's old pretentious tower, and the sound
of his leaping stream out-sings what my musings found.
Ballylee's here; and there, a mile off, lived
the Gregories. When troopers came by, Yeats grieved
that he could but dream what less brooding men achieved:
passionate action, that holds life and work spellbound—
real, murderous, even on this provincial ground.

From The View from the Peacock's Tail: Poems *by M. L. Rosenthal. Copyright © 1972 by M. L. Rosenthal. Reprinted by permission of Oxford University Press, Inc.*

Patrick J. Keane

Epilogue

I recently received M. L. Rosenthal's latest collection of poems, *The View from the Peacock's Tail,* and was deeply moved by a number of the poems, particularly by the last two. One of them, "Visiting Yeats's Tower," reprinted on the previous page, is based on an experience, the poet has told me, "in which I suddenly realized how it had felt to be Yeats in a certain frame of mind climbing up those stairs."

In the final poem of the collection, "Memory: A Meditation and a Quarrel with the Master," Rosenthal deals with love and death and finds he must "quarrel with the master's beloved words. Man never 'created death.'" The pronouncements of the master (Yeats), his celebration of friends in whose "lineaments" Irish history can be traced; the leaping of his symbolic swan "into the desolate heaven": against all these Rosenthal sets "Merely friends' faces. Little history knows or cares." We hear of an old man, a boarder, the poet's stepfather, textile strikers of 1928, the scattered "bones of men and women I loved." Called up, like ghosts in a number of Yeats's poems, they "make one reply: 'We died/before you could remember us again.'" The final movement stirs and mixes memories. It concludes with the modulation of the characteristic vocabulary of the distanced Yeats ("stare," "sky," "beautiful," "cold," "solitude") into the homely, humanistic message of the poet-son as well as of the mother:

> I stare at the sky
> that glows as beautiful, as cold, as true to solitude

as when my mother walked upon the earth and dreamed
of how, when a girl, she'd dreamed
of returning home to Jónava to tell the peasants:
"Love one another, and the Jews, and lovely books and thoughts."

The poem is, though lover's quarrel, quarrel nonetheless. It is—to quote from "Late at Night," the poem that supplies the title of his volume—Rosenthal's "brown-grey, barnyard-homey" view from the *back* of that glorious—and Yeatsian—peacock's tail. And if one looks again at the paragraph I excerpted from *The Ordinary Universe* to form the conclusion to the Donoghue essay, one will recognize the subtle entry of Ezra Pound into this confrontation between the bronzes of symbolism and the browns of reality.

I was moved by these poems to try to compose a kind of reply. Written in a stanza meant to recall Yeats's *ottava rima* (though a variant far less subtle and technically demanding than the aaabbbcc of "Visiting Yeats's Tower"), my poem (or pastiche) records an outburst in a pub during the 1972 Yeats International Summer School held in Sligo, Ireland.

The highlight of the conference, for me, was a lecture by the Ulster poet, Seamus Heaney. This lecture focused on the compassionate humanity—not the most characteristic gesture of the cold-eyed Yeats—of the final movement of "The Man and the Echo." In the poet's concern not with the violent hawk but with the stricken rabbit, Heaney found a point at which "Christ and Caesar are hand in glove" in Yeats's work. The fact that Heaney came from the strife-torn North, together with the pub incident noted in the first stanza, suggested a point of contact not only between Caesar and Christ but between Yeats and Joyce, specifically Joyce's Bloom, and, still more specifically, as he appears in the "Cyclops" episode of *Ulysses.* These thoughts floated in disconnection until the reading of *The View from the Peacock's Tail* brought them all together. These poems are printed here because they comment on the ambiguous legacy of Yeats; a man and poet whose human and visionary commitments, close and remote perspectives, are revealed in the essays selected for this volume. My own poem, which follows, may be thought of as little more than a coda to much of what has been said in prose in the preceding pages.

RECONCILIATION

–But it's no use, says he. Force, hatred, history, all that. That's not life for men and women, insult and hatred. And everybody knows that it's the very opposite of that that is life.

–What? says Alf.

–Love, says Bloom. I mean the opposite of hatred. I must go now. . . .

– . . . Your God was a jew. Christ was a jew like me. Gob, the citizen made a plunge back into the shop.

–By Jesus, says he, I'll brain that bloody jewman for using the holy name. By Jesus, I'll crucify him so I will. (Joyce)

God us keep/From single vision. . . . (Blake)

"'Yeats! YEATS!!' In the name of bleeding Jaysus
What kind of IRISH name d'ye call that!"
Loosed from a booze-flushed stupid face, mere words
Vomited over rotten yellow stumps:
A second coming, here, of Bloom's Cyclops,
That citizen in Joyce's book who spat
(He, with his mongrel and stone-age club)
Hate on the bestial floor of Kiernan's pub.

Though chauvinists in this blind bitter land
Felt Yeats's lash, they are at their old tricks yet.
Not–Poet and would-be Prophet (honored most
By tourists to that country)–not that *you*
(Who studied hatred with great diligence;
Owned yourself a biased man, and read
Mainly to confirm what you believed)
Had other than that "fanatic heart" you claimed:

"Out of Ireland have we come./Great hatred,
Little room. . . ." What flames upon the Northern night
Resinous hearts of stone have fed:
One eye, blank and pitiless, glaring hate.
As burning-mad and maimed, you fought it down;
Your choice, the student's lamp; their school, a crowd.
Yet your mysterious wisdom won by toil
Was the fruit of more, and less, than midnight oil.

Cast from those "gygantogyres" Joyce mocked,
That passionate cold eye burned ice. But mind,
Rapt in Byzantine simplicities
As mummies in the mummy-cloth are wound,
Might be distracted. Heaney dwelt upon
Such a moment in his Sligo talk:
"'A stricken rabbit is crying out,
And its cry distracts my thought.'"

You found, and were doubtless right to find,
"Christian love insufficient" to your need.
Brooding upon hawks and history, your mind,
Like a great-winged Bird or God above the stream,
Mounted to Vision; but the man retired
Behind a cloud to hone an indifferent beak.
Did you, in even the loftiest midnight hour,
Put on sufficient knowledge with your power?

You gazed, at times, in glory from that cloud;
Or from the Tower or the Boiler-top,
Chanting or ranting as the tidal blood,
Tormented or embittered by the moon,
Was caught, changed into changeless birds; or blocked
Myopic eye—blurring, troubling the sight.
Rough beasts moved in the deserts of your rage,
Or irrational streams of ink, to stain a page.

In the kingdom of the blind, the one-eyed man's. . .
"King of the cats," you gaily called yourself.
And though (at one with 'Poldy Bloom, for once)
You'd use for neither pub nor bully, we
Must with your greatness take your violence.
Still: no Cyclops in his "glory-hole," you'd laugh
To see love bloom, or pitch at least a tent,
In even that place of puke and excrement.

Force, hatred, history . . . in the name of Christ.
Earlier I'd asked an old man what he thought
Of this Yeats stuff. "Yeats? . . . Yeats. . . ." He sipped his pint.
"I can tell you one thing . . ." (his ancient eyes were gay)
". . . He never kicked football for Sligo!"
But gut-torn Ulster's poet said it best;
For those times, his "Christ and Caesar hand in glove,"
Yeats sang Bloom's opposite of hatred, love.

Selected Bibliography

I YEATS'S WORK

The following bibliography, though extensive, is far from complete. For the full record of Yeats's writings (and broadcasts), see *A Bibliography of the Writings of W. B. Yeats,* ed. Allan Wade, 3rd ed. revised and edited by Russell K. Alspach (Rupert-Hart Davis, London, 1968). Unless otherwise indicated, the publisher of the works of Yeats listed below is the Macmillan Company, New York. (I have tried, in the case of both primary and secondary works, to cite the editions most accessible to U.S. students.)

The central texts are of course *The Collected Poems of W. B. Yeats* ("Definitive Edition," 1956) and *The Collected Plays of W. B. Yeats* ("New Edition," 1953). The textual variants of the printed versions of all the poems and plays, as well as Yeats's (also much-revised) introductions and notes, have been collated in *The Variorum Edition of the Poems of W. B. Yeats,* ed. Peter Allt and Russell K. Alspach (1957), and *The Variorum Edition of the Plays of W. B. Yeats,* ed. Russell K. Alspach, assisted by Catherine Alspach (1966). While there is no substitute for the complete canon, an excellent selection is offered in M. L. Rosenthal, *Selected Poems and Two Plays of William Butler Yeats* (1962). Selections of poems, plays, and prose have been edited by A. N. Jeffares.

The bulk of the major prose is readily accessible in attractive (though not scholarly) reprint editions: *Mythologies* (1959), *Essays and Introductions* (1961), *Explorations* (1962), and *A Vision* ("A Re-issue With the Author's Final Revisions," 1961). The autobiographical writings appear as *The Autobiography of William Butler Yeats* (Anchor Doubleday, Garden City, N.Y., 1958). The major collection of correspondence is *The Letters of W. B. Yeats,* ed. Allan Wade (1954). Of several other sources the most important for readers of the poetry is *Letters on Poetry from W. B. Yeats to Dorothy Wellesley* (Oxford University Press, New York, 1940; reprinted, with an introduction by Kathleen Raine, 1964). A generous selection of speeches and critical reviews is offered in *The Senate Speeches of W. B. Yeats,* ed. Donald R. Pearce (Indiana University Press, Bloomington, 1960), and *Uncollected Prose by W. B. Yeats,* ed. John B. Frayne (Columbia University Press, New York, 1970), the first of two projected volumes. An early novel and story are now available in *John Sherman and Dhoya,* ed. Richard J. Finneran (Wayne State University Press, Detroit, 1969).

II SECONDARY WORKS

This bibliography is, with a handful of exceptions, restricted to volumes devoted wholly to Yeats. The inclusion of even the most important articles, background studies, and books dealing in part with Yeats would swell the list beyond tolerable limits.* Nor are all the full-volume studies of Yeats included below; emphasis is of course intended to fall on the best, the most influential, the more recent. For accounts of the Yeats industry's total output, see John E. Stoll, *The Great Deluge: A Yeats Bibliography* (Whitston, Troy, N.Y., 1971) and K. G. W. Cross and R. T. Dunlop, *A Bibliography of Yeats Criticism, 1887–1965,* with an Introduction by A. Norman Jeffares (Macmillan, London, 1971). These volumes may be supplemented by the annual *PMLA* bibliographies.

*The reader interested in tracking down these materials must be referred to volumes listed below, particularly the recent bibliographies. More accessible, though it does not go beyond 1950, is the "Select Bibliography" in *The Permanence of Yeats,* ed. Steinmann and Hall (pp. 349–77). This may be supplemented by the introductory matter to Saul's *Prolegomena* to the poems (pp. 15–30), Appendix II to the 1968 edition of Wade's bibliography (pp. 458–66), the "Select Reading List" in Rajan's *W. B. Yeats* (pp. 193–99), and the extensive bibliography in the Maxwell-Bushrui collection (*W. B. Yeats,* pp. 227–41). Annotated bibliographies may be found in J. I. M. Stewart, *Eight Modern Writers,* vol. XII of *The Oxford History of English Literature,* ed. F. P. Wilson and Bonamy Dobrée (Clarendon Press, Oxford, 1963, pp. 671–79), and *In Excited Reverie,* ed. A. N. Jeffares and K. G. W. Cross (pp. 315–37). Other surveys of Yeats criticism and research include (in chronological order): A. N. Jeffares, "An Account of Recent Yeatsiana," *Hermathena 72* (1948), 21–43; Hazard Adams, "Yeats Scholarship and Criticism: A Review of Research," *Texas Studies in Literature and Language 3* (1962), 439–51; George Mills Harper, "'All the Instruments Agree': Some observations on Recent Yeats Criticism," *Sewanee Review 74* (1966), 739–54; John Brian, "Hurt into Poetry: Some Recent Yeats Studies," *Journal of General Education 18* (1967), 299–306; Ian Fletcher, "History and Vision in the Work of W. B. Yeats," *Southern Review 4* (1968), 105–26; Hazard Adams, "Criticism, Politics, and History: The Matter of Yeats," *Georgia Review 24* (1970), 158–82; and George Mills Harper "'Sing Whatever is Well Made': Recent Books about Yeats," *CEA Critic 33* (1971), 29–35.

Collections

Donoghue, Denis, ed.: *The Integrity of Yeats,* Mercier Press, Cork, Ireland, 1964.

Donoghue, Denis, and J. R. Mulryne, eds.: *An Honoured Guest: New Essays on W. B. Yeats,* St. Martin's Press, New York, 1965.

Gordon, D. J., ed.: *W. B. Yeats: Images of a Poet,* Barnes and Noble, New York, 1961.

Gwynn, Stephen L., ed.: *William Butler Yeats: Essays in Tribute,* Kennikat Press, Port Washington, N.Y., 1965 (originally published as *Scattering Branches,* 1940).

Hall, James, and Martin Steinmann, eds.: *The Permanence of Yeats,* Macmillan, New York, 1950 (reprinted 1961).

Jeffares, A. Norman, and K. G. W. Cross, eds.: *In Excited Reverie: A Centenary Tribute to William Butler Yeats, 1865–1939,* New York, Macmillan, 1965.

MacManus, Francis, ed.: *The Yeats We Knew,* Mercier Press, Cork, Ireland, 1965.

Maxwell, D. E. S., and S. B. Bushrui, eds.: *W. B. Yeats, 1865–1965: Centenary Essays on the Art of W. B. Yeats,* Ibadan University Press, Ibadan, Nigeria, 1965 (available through International Publications Service, New York).

Miller, Liam, ed.: *Dolmen Press Yeats Centenary Papers, 1965,* Dolmen Press, Dublin, 1966.

Skelton, Robin, and Anne Saddlemyer, eds.: *The World of W. B. Yeats: Essays in Perspective,* Adelphi Bookshop for the University of Victoria, Victoria, British Columbia, 1965 (distributed in the U.S. by University of Washington Press, Seattle).

Stallworthy, Jon, ed.: *Yeats's Last Poems: A Casebook,* Macmillan, London, 1968.

Unterecker, John: *Yeats: A Collection of Critical Essays* (Twentieth Century Views Series), Prentice-Hall, Englewood Cliffs, N.J., 1963.

Other collections of critical essays have appeared in the form of "special issues" of periodicals. They include: *The Arrow* (Summer 1939); *Southern Review 7* (1942); *Irish Writing 31* (1955); *Review of English Literature 4* (1963); *Hermathena 101* (1965); *Phoenix* (Korea) *10* (1965); *University Review 3* (1965); *Tri-Quarterly 1* (1965); *James Joyce Quarterly 3* (1965); *Southern Review 5* (1969); *Ariel* (formerly *Review of English Literature*) (July 1972). In addition, Yeats now has his "own" magazine: *Yeats Studies: An International Journal* (Lorna Reynolds and Robert O'Driscoll, eds.) began publication in the spring of 1971.

Critical and Biographical Studies; Research Tools

Adams, Hazard: *Blake and Yeats: The Contrary Vision,* Cornell University Press, Ithaca, N.Y., 1955.

Albright, Daniel: *Myth Against Myth: A Study of Yeats's Imagination in Old Age,* Oxford University Press, New York, 1972.

Beum, Robert: *The Poetic Art of William Butler Yeats,* Frederick Ungar, New York, 1969.

Bjersby, Birgit: *Interpretations of the Cuchulain Legend in the Works of W. B. Yeats,* Harvard University Press, Cambridge, 1951.

Bloom, Harold: *Yeats,* Oxford University Press, New York, 1970.

Bornstein, George: *Yeats and Shelley,* University of Chicago Press, Chicago, 1970.

Bradford, Curtis B.: *Yeats at Work,* Southern Illinois University Press, Carbondale and Edwardsville, 1965.

Bushrui, S. B.: *Yeats's Verse Plays: The Revisions, 1900–1910,* Clarendon Press, Oxford, 1965.

Clark, David R.: *W. B. Yeats and the Theatre of Desolate Reality,* Dolmen Press, Dublin, 1965.

Cowell, Raymond: *W. B. Yeats,* Arco, New York, 1970.

Desai, Rupin W.: *Yeats's Shakespeare,* Northwestern University Press, Evanston, Ill., 1971.

Donogue, Denis: *William Butler Yeats,* Viking Press, New York, 1971.

Eddins, Dwight: *Yeats: The Nineteenth Century Matrix,* University of Alabama Press, 1971.

Ellmann, Richard: *Yeats: The Man and the Masks,* Macmillan, New York, 1948.

———: *The Identity of Yeats,* 2nd ed., Oxford University Press, New York, 1964 (1st ed., 1954).

———: *Eminent Domain: Yeats Among Wilde, Joyce, Pound, Eliot, and Auden,* Oxford University Press, New York, 1967.

Engelberg, Edward: *The Vast Design: Patterns in W. B. Yeats's Aesthetic,* University of Toronto Press, Toronto, 1965.

Fraser, G. S.: *W. B. Yeats,* Longmans, New York, 1962 (originally published 1954).

Garab, Arra M.: *Beyond Byzantium: The Last Phase of Yeats's Career,* Northern Illinois University Press, De Kalb, 1969.

Grossman, Allen R.: *Poetic Knowledge in the Early Yeats: A Study of the Wind Among the Reeds,* University of Virginia Press, Charlottesville, 1969.

Henn, T. R.: *The Lonely Tower: Studies in the Poetry of W. B. Yeats,* 2nd ed., Barnes and Noble, New York, 1965 (1st ed., 1950).

Hone, Joseph: *W. B. Yeats, 1865–1939,* 2nd ed., St. Martin's Press, New York, 1962; reprinted 1965 (1st ed., 1942).

Jeffares, A. Norman: *W. B. Yeats, Man and Poet,* 2nd ed., Barnes and Noble, New York, 1966 (1st ed., 1949).

———: *The Poems of W. B. Yeats,* Barron's Educational Series, Great Neck, N.Y., 1961.

———: *A Commentary on the Collected Poems of W. B. Yeats,* University of Stanford Press, Stanford, Calif., 1968.

———: *The Circus Animals: Essays on W. B. Yeats,* Macmillan, London, 1970.

Kermode, Frank: *Romantic Image,* Random House, New York, 1964 (originally published 1957).

Kirby, Sheilah, compiler, and P. Gallagher, ed.: *The Yeats Country,* Dolmen Press, Dublin, 1962.

Koch, Vivienne: *W. B. Yeats: The Tragic Phase,* Routledge and Kegan Paul, London, 1951.

Lentricchia, Frank: *The Gaiety of Language: An Essay on the Radical Poetics of W. B. Yeats and Wallace Stevens,* University of California Press, Berkeley and Los Angeles, 1968.

Levine, Bernard: *The Dissolving Image: The Spiritual-Esthetic Development of W. B. Yeats,* Wayne State University Press, Detroit, 1970.

MacLiammóir, Micheál, and Eavan Boland: *W. B. Yeats and His World,* Viking Press, New York, 1972.

MacNeice, Louis: *The Poetry of W. B. Yeats,* with a foreword by Richard Ellmann, Oxford University Press, New York, 1967 (originally published 1941).

Marcus, Philip L.: *Yeats and the Beginning of the Irish Renaissance,* Cornell University Press, Ithaca, N.Y., 1971.

Melchiori, Giorgio: *The Whole Mystery of Art: Pattern into Poetry in the Work of W. B. Yeats,* Macmillan, New York, 1961.

Menon, V. K. Narayana: *The Development of William Butler Yeats,* 2nd ed., Dufour, Philadelphia, 1961 (1st ed., 1942).

Moore, John Rees: *Masks of Love and Death: Yeats as Dramatist,* Cornell University Press, Ithaca, N.Y., 1971.

Moore, Virginia: *The Unicorn: William Butler Yeats's Search for Reality,* Macmillan, New York, 1954.

Nathan, Leonard E.: *The Tragic Drama of William Butler Yeats: Figures in a Dance,* Columbia University Press, New York, 1965.

Orel, Harold: *The Development of William Butler Yeats: 1885–1900,* University of Kansas Press, Lawrence, 1968.

Parkinson, Thomas: *W. B. Keats: Self-Critic and the Later Poetry,* University of California Press, Berkeley and Los Angeles,

1971 (combined edition of *W. B. Yeats: Self-Critic,* 1951, and *W. B. Yeats: The Later Poetry,* 1964).

Parrish, Stephen Maxfield, ed.: *A Concordance to the Poems of W. B. Yeats,* programmed by James Allan Painter, Cornell University Press, Ithaca, N.Y., 1963.

Perloff, Marjorie: *Rhyme and Meaning in the Poetry of Yeats,* Mouton, The Hague, 1970.

Rajan, Balachandra: *W. B. Yeats: A Critical Introduction,* Hillary House, New York, 1965.

Reid, Benjamin L.: *W. B. Yeats: The Lyric of Tragedy,* University of Oklahoma Press, Norman, 1961.

Ronsley, Joseph: *Yeats's Autobiography: Life as Symbolic Pattern,* Harvard University Press, Cambridge, 1968.

Saul, George Brandon: *Prolegomena to the Study of Yeats's Poems,* University of Pennsylvania Press, Philadelphia, 1957.

———: *Prolegomena to the Study of Yeats's Plays,* University of Pennsylvania Press, Philadelphia, 1958.

Seiden, Morton Irving: *William Butler Yeats: The Poet as a Mythmaker, 1865–1939,* Michigan State University Press, East Lansing, 1962.

Sidnell, Michael J., *et al: Druid Craft; The Writing of The Shadowy Waters,* University of Massachusetts Press, Amherst,1972.

Stallworthy, Jon: *Between the Lines: Yeats's Poetry in the Making,* Clarendon Press, Oxford, 1963.

———; *Visions and Revisions in Yeats's Last Poems,* Clarendon Press, Oxford, 1969.

Stauffer, Donald A.: *The Golden Nightingale,* Macmillan, New York, 1949.

Stock, A. G.: *W. B. Yeats: His Poetry and Thought,* Cambridge University Press, Cambridge, 1961.

Tindall, William York: *W. B. Yeats* (Essays on Modern Writers, no. 15), Columbia University Press, New York, 1966.

Torchiana, Donald: *W. B. Yeats and Georgian Ireland,* Northwestern University Press, Evanston, Ill., 1966.

Unterecker, John: *A Reader's Guide to William Butler Yeats,* Noonday Press, New York, 1959.

Ure, Peter: *Towards a Mythology: Studies in the Poetry of W. B. Yeats,* University Press of Liverpool, Liverpool, 1946.

———: *Yeats the Playwright: A Commentary on Character and Design in the Major Plays,* Barnes and Noble, New York, 1963.

———: *W. B. Yeats,* Grove Press, New York, 1964.

Veeder, William R.: *W. B. Yeats: The Rhetoric of Repetition,* University of California Press, Berkeley and Los Angeles, 1968.

Vendler, Helen Hennessy: *Yeats's "Vision" and the Later Plays,* Harvard University Press, Cambridge, 1963.

Whitaker, Thomas R.: *Swan and Shadow: Yeats's Dialogue with History,* University of North Carolina Press, Chapel Hill, 1964.

Wilson, F. A. C.: *W. B. Yeats and Tradition,* Macmillan, New York, 1958.

———: *Yeats's Iconography,* Victor Gollancz, London, 1960.

Winters, Yvor: *The Poetry of W. B. Yeats* (Swallow Pamphlets, no. 10), Allen Swallow, Denver, 1960.

Zwerdling, Alex: *Yeats and the Heroic Ideal,* New York University Press, New York, 1965.

III A NOTE ON THE BIBLIOGRAPHY

How does the student new to Yeats thread his way through this labyrinth? A few rough notes may help. He begins with Yeats; with the poems first, then the plays. The author himself provides "A General Introduction for my Work" and "An Introduction for my Plays" (both in *Essays and Introductions*). For additional assistance, see Yeats's introductions and notes to the poems and plays in the variorum editions, Saul's two volumes of prolegomena, and (for the poems only) Jeffares's *Commentary* and Unterecker's *Reader's Guide.* Of Yeats's more formal prose the student can least afford to neglect the *Autobiography, Per Amica Silentia Lunae* (in *Mythologies*), and, from *A Vision,* the "Introduction," the opening sections of "A Great Wheel" (pp. 67–89), and "Dove or Swan."

The secondary literature is so vast that no brief guide can be other than prejudiced. The following paragraphs must be taken as reflecting both received opinion and personal experience.

Hone's biography, still important, should be supplemented by the opening chapter of Henn's *The Lonely Tower;* Jeffares's *W. B. Yeats, Man and Poet;* Ellmann's *Yeats: The Man and the Masks;* and Wade's edition of the *Letters.* Perhaps the best brief introductions are those by Fraser and Rosenthal. Stock, Reid, Rajan, and Ure *(W. B. Yeats)* offer lucid guides for the general reader. Also covering the whole of Yeats's work are *The Permanence of Yeats* and the most illuminating of the critical collections, *An Honoured Guest.*

The most judicious balance between general and specialist studies has been attained by Ellmann. *The Man and the Masks,* centering on the multi-faceted personality behind the work, and

The Identity of Yeats, stressing the underlying thematic unity of the work itself, remain at the vital center of Yeats criticism. Almost as crucial are Parkinson's *Self-Critic* and *The Later Poetry,* examinations, respectively, of the early and later poems, both in the process of composition and as finished artifacts.

There are, in addition to Kermode's *Romantic Image,* a number of excellent specialist studies. Engelberg offers a lucid exposition of the aesthetic theory upon which the poems are based. Melchiori, expanding T. R. Henn's emphasis on visual sources of Yeats's imagery, focuses on the mental process through which certain dominant images coalesce into poetry. Torchiana richly documents the poet's ties, of blood and spirit, to the Anglo-Irish eighteenth century. Vendler reads twelve later plays from the symbolic and theoretical perspective of *A Vision.* Wilson, in two controversial exegeses, interprets Yeats's work in the light of the symbolism of the occult-Neoplatonic "Tradition," relegating un-Traditional imagery to mere decoration.

Sophisticated, comprehensive command of the whole body of literature by, about, and influencing Yeats is most impressively displayed in Whitaker's *Swan and Shadow* and Bloom's *Yeats.* Bloom's important book (which should have been given some such title as *Yeats and the Romantic Legacy*) rightly insists on the poet's consciousness of his role in the tradition of apocalyptic romanticism; but it also labels every deviation from Blake and Shelley a betrayal—as though Yeats were somehow not entitled to a "vision" of his own.

Other important volumes could be mentioned—and there are still more on the horizon. John Kelly and Eric Domville are presently engaged in compiling a comprehensive edition of Yeats's letters. (Domville has just completed a concordance to the plays.) Other expected books, incorporating much unpublished material, include a full-scale study by George Mills Harper of Yeats and the occult and an examination of Yeats in the context of the western philosophical tradition by Donald Torchiana. M. L. Rosenthal is re-examining Yeats in connection with Pound and Eliot. The actual *dramatis personae,* the real people who appear in or inform Yeats's work, will be discussed by Lester Connor. Perhaps the most important of these, the poet's father, is the subject of a massive forthcoming biography by William M. Murphy. Finally, as the present volume is being set, Yeatsians are eagerly awaiting the soon-to-be published book by Denis Donoghue—a full-scale, authorized biography which promises to answer many questions, open many others, and almost certainly set in motion a new wave of critical assessment and evaluation.

Catalog

If you are interested in a list of fine Paperback books, covering a wide range of subjects and interests, send your name and address, requesting your free catalog, to:

McGraw-Hill Paperbacks
1221 Avenue of Americas
New York, N.Y. 10020

PB-367-1
5-13